MW01245823

ACCIDENTS IN
NORTH AMERICAN
MOUNTAINEERING

1991

ACCIDENTS IN NORTH AMERICAN MOUNTAINEERING

VOLUME 6 • NUMBER 2 • ISSUE 44

1991

THE AMERICAN ALPINE CLUB
NEW YORK

THE ALPINE CLUB OF CANADA
BANFF

© 1991 The American Alpine Club, Inc.

All rights reserved. No part of this publication may be reproduced or transmitted in any form or by any means, electronic or mechanical, including photocopy, recording, or any information and retrieval systems, without permission from the publisher.

ISSN 0065-082X

ISBN 930410-47-5

Manufactured in the United States of America

Published by
The American Alpine Club, Inc.
133 East 90th Street
New York, New York 10128-1589

Cover Illustration
Photograph of an injured climber who had just been sling-loaded under a Bell helicopter from Mount Teewinot to Lupine Meadows in Grand Teton National Park. His knee "locked up" while descending, so he was unable to walk. His partner ran to the valley and contacted the Park Rangers. The victim was impressed with the rescue, especially the rest of his descent! Photograph by John E. (Jed) Williamson.

SAFETY COMMITTEES 1991

The American Alpine Club

Dr. Benjamin G. Ferris, Jr., John Dill, Fred Stanley, Rick Wilcox, James Yester, and John E. (Jed) Williamson *(Chairman)*

The Alpine Club of Canada

Ian Findlay, Helmut Microys, Orvel Miskiw, Paul Ritzema, and Murray Toft *(Chairman)*

CONTENTS

ACCIDENTS IN
NORTH AMERICAN MOUNTAINEERING

Forty-Fourth Annual Report of the
Safety Committees of The American Alpine Club
and The Alpine Club of Canada

This is the forty-fourth issue of *Accidents in North American Mountaineering* and the thirteenth that has been done jointly by the American Alpine Club and The Alpine Club of Canada.

Canada: Several of the accidents in 1990 involved solo climbers, though not all of those can fairly be attributed to the soloing: some victims would likely have been in the same situation even with partners along. However, the usual loose understanding that "soloing" means "without partners" is often not the point at all, as an unroped climber who falls off a ledge or 30 meters down a crevasse to bedrock is hardly better off with a partner nearby than if he had been "soloing" (by that definition). On the other hand, soloists sometimes belay themselves, and if this is done correctly, it is vastly safer than being in an unroped party in the same terrain. In the accident sense, solo-type climbing includes most solo climbers plus all those in groups who are unprotected while exposed, and that is a dominant factor in climbing accidents. Of the five deaths reported this year, four were unroped, and the fifth was roped but not belayed. Of the remaining accidents, one involved rockfall, four were a result of inadequate protection or anchoring, four came from being roped but not belayed, and the rest were a result of not being roped up. Most of the accidents could have been averted or lessened by better protection.

We thank Tim Auger, George Field, Clair Israelson, Ian Kay, B. Kozachenko, Marc Ledwidge, Rick Ralf, Fred Stanley, and Lee Tibbert for submitting reports, and all the others who fortunately either had nothing to report, or whose reports did not fit our mountaineering criteria.

United States: "Two *are* better than one; because they have good reward for their labor. For if they fall, the one will lift up his fellow: but woe to him that is alone when he falleth; for he hath not another to help him up." (Ecclesiastes, 4: 9 & 10) Now if some reference to the use of "adequate protection" could be found in this same—or an equivalent—source, the great percentage of preventive measures for this year's contributory causes to climbing injuries and fatalities would be neatly summarized. Placing proper protection seems to be a continuing problem, and may have something to do with the proliferation of different kinds of devices for that purpose—as well as the increase in levels of route difficulty being attempted. But the rise in the injury and fatality rate which was the direct result of not wearing a helmet is somewhat bewildering. There are climbing areas where the use of head gear is recognized as an extremely good idea because of the geology, the routes, and the numbers of climbers in the same vicinity. Yet these are the very places where the increase happened. Woe to him who hath no roof over his head when projectiles rain down, or when he flieth down a rock face unexpectedly...

There were some other interesting mountain related accidents which did not make the data or the narratives this year. Ken Phillips, the SAR Specialist in Grand Canyon National Park, sent four reports of accidents requiring rescue on technical rock terrain. Two cases involved stranded scramblers, with no injuries. The other two, which resulted in fatalities, were solo "climbers" (one in sandals) who had not indicated to anyone that they were going to engage in that activity. One was a member of a river trip, and it was reported that he was "fascinated by the sport." He had done many other short, free-solo climbs along the way before his twelve meter fall from a chimney. Again, these are the kinds of accidents which make the media with headlines accusing or at least implicating our sport as being the culprit.

One of the more interesting set of headlines this year included these: "Suspect tells his version of fatal fall. Wife excited about rappel try, he says;" and, "Wife's policies bought jointly, says man accused in fatal fall." This was a case where a man was accused of putting his wife in harm's way when he took her rappelling one evening and the anchor system he'd set up failed. He was eventually convicted of criminally negligent homicide. For more details, consult *The News Tribune*, Tacoma, WA, 2, 19-23, 1991.

The method of injured and deceased climber recovery shown on the front cover this year is becoming more prominent in certain geographic locations now. At a recent International Congress on Mountain Medicine held in Switzerland, I learned that out of Zermatt alone, there are 800 helicopter recoveries per year, and a doctor is in attendance every time. The rescue station there garages four helicopters, and the average time for delivery of a victim to a medical facility is twenty minutes from the time of call in. Every citizen pays an annual obligatory fee of twenty Swiss francs for this service, which has come to be a "standard" in the Alps. While the "insurance" is cheap, the fact is that people have come to count on—and expect—this kind of fast squad. There is certainly a great difference between rescue attitudes and services here and there. The question of climbers—and all backcountry users—taking responsibility for their own safety, care, and rescue was debated at the Congress, and must continue to be a topic of consideration for us all.

In addition to the Safety Committee, we are grateful to the following individuals for collecting data and helping with the report: Peter Armington, Dennis Burge, Micki Canfield, David Essex, Erik Hansen, Bob Siebert, Thomas Sheuer, and Reed Thorne. George Sainsbury tried to retire, but couldn't resist being of help, as usual.

John E. (Jed) Williamson
Editor, USA
7 River Ridge
Hanover, NH 03755

Orvel Miskiw
Editor, Canada
8631 - 34th Ave NW
Calgary, Alberta T3B 1R5

CANADA

FALL ON ICE, ROPED BUT NOT BELAYED
Alberta, Rocky Mountains, Mount Aberdeen

The initial pitches of the North Glacier route of Mount Aberdeen consist of 35-degree ice, usually bare in summer. On July 14, 1990, two climbers were roped together and moving simultaneously up this section without protection when the lower one lost a crampon, slipped, and pulled his partner from his stance. They fell about 65 meters and stopped in the rocks below. One of them sustained an ankle fracture while the other sustained ankle and wrist fractures. The latter lowered his partner to a more comfortable position and then retraced the approach to summon help. After about five hours of hobbling, he came across a hiking party; they went out and reported the accident. Both victims were rescued later that day by the Banff Warden Service.

Analysis

It should be recognized that, on even 'moderately' steep ice, it is very difficult to arrest a fall, particularly when roped to another climber. If the use of the rope is required, then the use of a proper anchor and belay is probably also required. (Source: Marc Ledwidge, Warden Service, Banff National Park)

AVALANCHE, INADEQUATE PREPARATION AND ROUTE SELECTION
Alberta, Rocky Mountains, Mount Andromeda

The morning of September 4, 1990, dawned with pristine clarity in the Columbia Ice-fields area. R.D. and J.E., both of Salt Lake City, Utah, had just arrived to do some ice climbing and were already en route to "Photo Finish," a smear of ice on the northeast face of Mount Andromeda, when the first rays of sun began to hit the ice-capped peaks. At 0930, climbing roped but unprotected through the center of the "Big Bowl" of Andromeda, the climbers were just approaching the bergschrund below the left of the base of their climb when the snow cracked above and around J.E., who was in the lead. Carried along helpless by the flow, he was just able to glimpse his partner scrambling to reach the right margin of the slide before he himself was tumbled over a crevasse and jerked to a sudden stop, on top and alert. J.D. was nowhere in sight. Climbing back to the edge of the crevasse he had just flown over, J.E. realized the reason for his abrupt halt: about two meters down was a ledge piled with snow into which the other end of his rope disappeared—one climbing boot protruded from the pile. J.E. was able to dig out and revive his partner, but R.D. was in no condition to travel. J.E. left him anchored to the crevasse wall and went for help, contacting the Parks Service at noon.

R.D. was reached by helicopter at 1351 and evacuated by HFRS (slinging) techniques at 1429. Six hours after his accident, he was being treated for hypothermia and badly frost-bitten hands in the hospital in Jasper.

Analysis

During the first two days of September, over 30 cm of snow fell at upper elevations in the Columbia Icefield area. The icy summit of 3450 meter Mount Andromeda had been lashed by gale-force winds during the latter part of that storm. Ridges and faces had been largely cleared of the new snow, but a drift slab had formed in the more protected area of the bowl, and it was resting on a hardened base.

The climbers had started early, not speaking to Park staff about past or present conditions, not wanting to wait for the opening of the information office at 0900, lest the promise of a spectacular day be lost. Though both of them were familiar with waterfall ice, neither listed winter mountaineering in his experience. Had they been aware of recent conditions, or had they spoken to someone more knowledgeable of alpine ice or potential hazards, they may not have chosen the fresh snow field in the center of the bowl as their approach to the climb, an approach also exposed to an overhanging bulge of ice. (Source: Clair Israelson, Canadian Parks Service)

FALL INTO CREVASSE, UNROPED, PUBLIC ON GLACIER
Alberta, Rocky Mountains, Athabasca Glacier

July 25, 1990, was a warm, sunny day, as a family of four from Calgary, Alberta, stopped at the Columbia Icefields in Jasper National Park and took a walk on the Athabasca Glacier. The oldest child, Tyson (10), was lightly dressed. About 1700, he ran out ahead of his parents and disappeared; he had slipped and fallen into a tapering crack and become wedged about three meters from the surface. His father ran for assistance and located a guided walking tour on the ice. The group leader returned to the crevasse with the father, set two ice screws as an anchor, and lowered himself. Being larger than the boy, he could not descend quite as far as him, but was able to secure a rope onto one of his ankles. Returning to the surface, the guide attempted, with the father, to pull the boy out, but the pressures involved caused Tyson to scream in pain, so this method of extrication was abandoned.

Park wardens were contacted at 1730, and the boy was removed, unconscious, from the crevasse, at 1848. Continuous resuscitation efforts at the scene, and later advanced life support, were unable to revive him. He was pronounced dead at 0200 the following morning.

Analysis

Hundreds of carefree tourists walk past warning signs at the toe of this glacier every year, and wander around on the surface of the ice without incident. To the general public it seems to be a straightforward and harmless activity requiring no special equipment or expertise, but a simple slip on the ice is all that was necessary to turn the natural exuberance of a child into a family tragedy. (Source: Clair Israelson, Canadian Parks Service)

(Editor's Note: This accident is not included in the data, but a discussion of how it could have been prevented quickly becomes a philosophic debate on individual rights and responsibilities, and the purposes of a National Park. It seems that when visitors ignore warning signs, they take on themselves the responsibility for their own safety. In Jasper National Park, which contains innumerable hazards, the only practical alternative to warning signs and notices might be to close the entire park to visitors. If closure cannot be considered, then visitors will have to be more careful.)

FALL ON ROCK, INSUFFICIENT PROTECTION
Alberta, Rocky Mountains, Barrier Bluffs

While leading the route called Cadillac Jack on June 3, 1990, T.C. fell and struck a ledge. Her partner lowered her to the ground, where it was obvious she had severely injured her right ankle. Numerous other climbers assisted the victim, applying a splint and giving her three tablets of a pain killer. The accident was reported to Kananaskis Rangers by phone from Barrier Information Centre at 1735. Rangers arrived at the accident site at 1810 and prepared T.C. for ground evacuation by Cascade stretcher (normally a half-hour walk on the narrow downhill trail through rubble and forest), but requested helicopter evacuation about 1825, as the victim was in extreme pain and showing symptoms of shock.

A machine from Canadian Helicopters was dispatched to the area via Bow Valley Provincial Park, and a ranger was slung to the accident site at 1920 for an aerial pick-up. The victim was lowered to a Barrier Lake parking area at 1930 and attended by medical personnel before transfer to an ambulance for transport to Calgary. It reached Foothills Hospital at 2000 and T.C.'s injuries were confirmed as a fracture and dislocation of the right ankle.

Analysis

There may be a tendency, especially among new climbers, to overestimate the powers of the rope. In this case, the overall protection system was inadequate to prevent a severe and extremely troublesome injury. (Source: George Field, Alpine Specialist, Peter Lougheed Provincial Park)

FALL ON SNOW AND ROCK
Alberta, Rocky Mountains, Mount Blakiston

On July 7, 1990, a party of five climbed the Class 4 south gully on Mount Blakiston. They were beginning their descent by traversing a small, moderately angled slope when the leader slipped and slid 15 meters into rocks, suffering a broken tibia and several gashes and contusions. With the help of his group, he was able to continue the 1000-meter descent to the valley trail. One person had been sent ahead to alert the Waterton Warden Service, who then completed the evacuation, using a wheeled mountain stretcher.

Analysis

More snow existed on this route than has been the norm for that time of year. The group carried ice axes, but no ropes or crampons, and did not appear to be aware of the immediate consequences of a fall on steep snow. By avoiding the snowfields, or being prepared to self-arrest, they may have prevented the accident. (Source: B. Kozachenko, Warden Service, Waterton Lakes National Park)

ANCHOR FAILURE WHILE LOWERING OFF
Alberta, Rocky Mountains, Cascade Mountain

During a climb of Mother's Day (5.6) in April, 1990, the leader placed a Friend and used it to lower back down. This anchor pulled out and he fell about three meters to a ledge, sustaining a broken ankle. He was grabbed by a companion and saved from a much longer fall. A third member of the party rappelled off and scrambled down for help.

Analysis
The failure here was in not ensuring that the single anchor was adequate. There is much evidence that extra care must be taken in placing Friends. (Source: T. Auger, Banff Warden Service)

FALL ON ROCK, PROTECTION PULLED OUT, INEXPERIENCE
Alberta, Rocky Mountains, Cascade Mountain
In July, 1990, a climber (19) fell while leading on cliffs just left of the Cascade waterfall. His first protection, a Friend, pulled out. The next one, a chock, held, but the victim fell about ten meters onto 60 degree rock, breaking a wrist and an ankle. His belayer lowered him to a ledge and went for help.

Analysis
The place where this party got into trouble has often fooled inexperienced climbers before: easy slabs gradually steepen and the rock is loose. The climbers had just purchased a load of brand new equipment. Their previous experience was limited mostly to artificial climbing walls in the city. (Source: T. Auger, Warden Service, Banff National Park)

STRANDED, SOLO ICE CLIMBING
Alberta, Rocky Mountains, Cascade Mountain
In December, 1990, a climber went to solo the Cascade waterfall when his partner decided not to go with him; temperatures were around -25C. He took a rope along, but his partner had told him the descent was a walk-off, so he left it at the base. He climbed the first steep pitch but balked at the top one; this left him stranded on a ledge. After several hours he was able to attract the attention of someone below, who then went for help. Rescuers climbed up in the dark and lowered the subject, who suffered frostbite of his feet.

Analysis
With the temperature reaching -35C that night, the simple decision to leave the rope behind could have been fatal. Even in solo climbing, a rope may be essential to a safe retreat if something comes up in mid-climb. In this case, the information that the descent is a walk-off was also wrong. (Source: T. Auger, Warden Service, Banff National Park)

(*Editor's Note: He could see the climb and assess the prospects for descent from where he left the rope, so he must have intended to cross over from the top and descend Rogan's Gully, as the Cascade is flanked by steep walls. He did not allow for the possibility of finding the upper pitch more difficult than the lower, and the lower one not feasible to downclimb.*)

FALL IN CREVASSE, UNROPED
Alberta, Rocky Mountains, French Glacier
A party of three was traveling, unroped, down the French Glacier on the morning of August 13, 1990, when one of them, D.D., fell into a crevasse. He was unable to extri-

cate himself, but managed to hook the lip of the crevasse with his ice ax for support while his two companions set up an anchor to hold him in place. Then one of them tended the anchor, and the other called for help with a radio which the victim had been carrying. Peter Lougheed Provincial Park officials got the call at 1300, and a ranger rescue party was sent to the Burstall Lakes parking lot, where they were met by a Canadian Helicopters unit at 1320. The rescuers and equipment were quickly flown to the accident site, where the victim was found to be too cold to assist them with his rescue. Additional anchors were established, and D.H. was extricated within ten minutes, then flown down to the parking lot, where he was transferred to an ambulance for transport to Canmore General Hospital. His injuries were bruises, cuts, scratches, and hypothermia.

Analysis
The party was led by a person who had knowledge of the area and was experienced in mountain travel, but the severity of crevassing is greatly underestimated by many travelers of the French-Haig-Robertson area. As well, strong winds had blown fine gravel over the upper section of the glacier, making detection of crevasses very difficult at ground level. This combination of factors resulted in D.H. misjudging his position. His fall into the unexpected hole and the absence of a rope resulted in exacerbating the situation. (Source: George Field, Alpine Specialist, Peter Lougheed Provincial Park)

(Editor's Note: Other than the use of a rope, the only divider between safety and serious trouble would be a solid snow plug not too many meters down, or a crevasse so narrow that one only goes a short distance and can use chimney techniques to ascend. This group did not have crampons. Either a rope or crampons, or better still, both, may have made self-rescue feasible, and correct use of the rope would have made rescue unnecessary. To their credit, the radio may have saved a life, but it is no substitute for basic safety gear.)

LOOSE ROCK
Alberta, Rocky Mountains, Grand Sentinel
The Grand Sentinel is a 100 meter quartzite pillar on the north slopes of Pinnacle Mountain, and Sentinel Pass which joins it to the southwest corner of Mount Temple. On August 11, 1990, two ACC rope teams were climbing different routes on this spire when the second climber, on the 5.6 north route, pulled off a large rock with his left hand. The rock fell on his right hand, breaking two fingers.

The first-aid supplies were in packs at the bottom of the Sentinel, but the victim still had the use of his thumb and first two fingers, and so was able to complete the pitch before his companions immobilized the affected hand with a bandanna. The party then traversed around the pillar to find a fixed rappel route, where the victim was lowered to 'terra firma.' He walked out with the rest of the party (a bit shaky on rough ground, with one hand in a sling) and was treated at Mineral Springs Hospital in Banff. Unfortunately, he eventually lost one of the injured fingers. (Source: Allan Main, ACC Calgary Section)

Analysis
Occasionally objective hazards strike without warning, but in this case the leader had warned the others about a rock which the second pulled out. The second may have

avoided the accident by watching for the loose rock as he followed up the pitch, and avoiding it when he found it. Also, a leader should make a special point of warning less experienced climbers about hazards which they may not recognize. (Source: Orvel Miskiw, AAC Calgary Section)

LOOSE ROCK, UNROPED FALL
Alberta, Rocky Mountains, Grassi Lakes area
While hiking with friends near Canmore on September 22, 1990, Mark undertook some solo climbing on the rock faces next to the second lake. He was about three meters off the ground when a handhold broke. He fell to the ground, turning around on the way, and injured his left leg as he landed on the sloping surface. His friends called Bow Valley Ambulance at 1350, and park rangers were asked to assist at the accident scene. An ambulance was able to reach the lake by using the Trans Alta Utilities service road, and the victim was attended by a paramedic and the ambulance crew before being moved to the ambulance with the assistance of Ranger S. The evacuation was complete by 1450. Mark's injury was diagnosed as a compound multiple fracture of the left tibia and fibula. (Source: George Field, Alpine Specialist, Peter Lougheed Provincial Park)

Analysis
A seemingly innocent diversion took a nasty turn in this case because of the coincidence of a number of unfavorable factors with the victim's heavy reliance on luck (by having no protection), being too high off the ground, having a handhold fail, twisting during the fall, and, landing on a sloping surface. Since the outing began as a hike, perhaps he was not mentally prepared or committed to climbing. (Source: Orvel Miskiw, ACC Calgary Section)

FALL ON ROCK, NO PROTECTION
Alberta, Rocky Mountains, Grotto Creek
On May 20, 1990, W.M. fell while climbing on Grotto Slabs, sustaining cuts, scrapes, and bruises to his left hand, right thigh, and the right side of his rib cage. He continued climbing for a while, before leaving with his companions to see whether a cut in his hand needed stitching. (Source: George Field, Alpine Specialist, Peter Lougheed Provincial Park)

STRANDED, CLIMBING ALONE, FAILURE TO TEST HOLD—FALLING ROCK, UNROPED
Alberta, Rocky Mountains, Grotto Canyon
On August 4, 1990, off-duty ranger M.S. was climbing with a partner in Grotto Canyon, when they found D.K. stranded on a ledge some 20 meters up the face of the His and Hers waterfalls. D.K. requested help in getting down, as he had pulled a rock loose while climbing, and sustained a swollen lip and minor abrasions. M.S. and his partner climbed the 5.4 pitch, improvised a harness for D.K., and belayed him to the bottom of the face. (Source: George Field, Alpine Specialist, Peter Lougheed Provincial Park)

SLIP ON SNOW, INAPPROPRIATE EQUIPMENT/TECHNIQUE
Alberta, Rocky Mountains, Mount Lefroy
On the morning of July 7, 1990, a party of two were descending the west face of Mount Lefroy, unroped. While glissading, sitting and wearing crampons, one of them accelerated out of control. One of his crampons caught in the snow, flipping him over and fracturing his ankle. He then managed to self-arrest and was helped down to Abbot Pass hut by his partner. The injured climber was airlifted from the hut later that morning by the Banff Warden Service.

Analysis
Ankle fractures are common in falls on snow and ice with crampons as they are not suitable for sliding. It is generally better to not wear them while glissading, since the use of feet is required for sliding and for self-arrest. (Source: Marc Ledwidge, Warden Service, Banff National Park)

FALL ON ROCK, INADEQUATE PROTECTION—ROPE ON TAPE, INEXPERIENCE
Alberta, Rocky Mountains, Rock Gardens (Jasper)
On April 5, 1990, around 1630, two climbers, Sean (17) and David (23), ventured off the Rock Gardens, a rock outcrop popular with the locals, and established a top rope at an existing two-bolt anchor. The rope was passed through a carabiner which allowed both the climber and the belayer to work from the bottom of the 25-meter bluff. Sometime later it was decided to move to a different location. Sean climbed to the anchor and, acting on the advice of David, removed the carabiner and threaded the rope directly through the remaining tape sling attached to the bolts. Sean was then lowered down the cliff face until the anchor sling melted through. A ten-meter fall resulted, and he sustained a severe pelvic injury.

David covered Sean, then raced out and reported the accident to Jasper Warden Service. Sean was established and evacuated by stretcher to a waiting ambulance.

Analysis
Feeding a rope through a sling should only be considered for a static situation, and even then only if no metal ring is available. (Source: Rick Ralf, Canadian Parks Service, Jasper)

FALL ON AVALANCHE DEBRIS, FATIGUE
Alberta, Rocky Mountains, Mount Rundle
On March 10, 1990, after completing ice climbs of Professor's Gully and Under the Volcano, Greg G. was descending the slopes of Mount Rundle, which are broken by cliff bands. He removed his crampons to downclimb the first cliff and continued easily down avalanche debris toward the second, where the slope dropped away toward a narrow gully.

As Greg moved to the edge of the debris to avoid the gully by continuing his descent among the trees, he lost his footing, was unable to stop, and fell down the gully. As he collided with its rock wall on his way to the hard slope 20 meters below, his helmet and one pack strap were torn off, and one arm was badly injured. He secured his arm inside a triangular bandage and his pile jacket, and began an arduous two-hour hike to the golf course, where he caught a ride to Mineral Springs Hospital in Banff. His injuries were a clean midshaft humerus fracture and a severe compound distal radius fracture.

Analysis
Greg feels he should have put his crampons back on, and that his mental concentration wavered while he was in an exposed position. He reflected that, "A climb isn't over 'til it's over." (Source: Greg S.)

FALL ON ROCK, UNROPED
Alberta, Rocky Mountains, Mount Rundle
In July, 1990, Martin (20) was scrambling unroped on slabs several hundred meters above the practice area on the east face of Mount Rundle when he fell, apparently at least 50 meters. His body was found after he was reported missing by friends.

Analysis
It is most likely that Martin, an inexperienced rock climber, got into trouble while trying out the new high performance rock shoes he had just purchased at a local store that morning. (Source: T. Auger, Banff Warden Service)

FAILURE TO TEST PROTECTION, ANCHOR SLING FAILURE, FALL ON ROCK
Alberta, Rocky Mountains, Spray Slabs
Spray Slabs is a practice area near Banff. In July, 1990, a leader (46) climbed a short distance above his belayer, clipped into a very old 9 mm webbing sling on a piton, and committed his weight to it. The knot held, but the sling broke and the victim fell, bounced off a narrow ledge, and landed on a wider ledge. He suffered bruises and a broken ankle.

Analysis
An existing anchor, especially a sling, is always suspect and relied on. (Source: T. Auger, Warden Service, Banff National Park)

FALL ON SNOW AND ICE, NO BELAY
Alberta, Rocky Mountains, Mount Temple
On August 1, 1990, a party of two climbed the Aemmer) snow couloir variant to the East Ridge route on Mount Temple and scouted out the rest of the route. Because of deteriorating weather, they decided to retreat down the couloir. They were wet and cold. They rappelled the upper third without incident, and then continued by downclimbing with 50 meters of rope before them, using crampons and ice axes. The 45-degree snow was becoming saturated with rain.

The higher climber fell and slid twice the rope length, where he was stopped by his partner, who then yelled for him to anchor himself and relieve the weight on the rope. When the fallen climber did not respond, the one holding the rope tried to move down to relieve the tension on it, which he could barely support. He lost control, and both climbers fell another 60 to 100 meters.

Both survived the fall and the night, but in the morning the one who fell originally was in critical condition. His partner crawled to him to anchor him to rocks and adjust his position, but despite his efforts, the first one died around noon that day. Around 1430, a wet snow avalanche carried his body another 50 meters down the gully, while the survivor managed to hang on to rocks and avoid further injury.

The climbers had registered with the Banff Warden Service and became overdue the next morning. Soon after that, the survivor was rescued and his friend's body recovered.

Analysis
It is not known why the first climber fell initially. His partner was fortunate to be able to arrest the fall, and it is thought that the rope dragging through snow runnels may have helped him. Other than belaying, moving together with only a meter of rope between them or continuing to rappel may have prevented serious injury during a fall. (Source: Marc Ledwidge, Warden Service, Banff National Park)

SLIP ON SCREE AND ROCK, UNPROTECTED
Alberta, Rocky Mountains, Mount Temple
On August 13, 1990, a lone climber was descending the "tourist route" on Mount Temple. It is speculated that he went slightly off route at the grey cliff band where the scree trails branch off in various directions, slipped on scree overlying bedrock, and fell down cliffs approximately 65 meters. Another party later discovered his body and reported to the Banff Warden Service. They evacuated the body the same day.

Analysis
Although this is a fairly easy descent route, it requires knowledge of route-finding skills through dangerous terrain. (Source: Marc Ledwidge, Warden Service, Banff National Park)

FALL INTO CREVASSE, UNROPED
Alberta, Rocky Mountains, Mount White Pyramid
Early in February, 1990, ten members of the ACC Calgary Section set off to try a winter ascent of White Pyramid (3277 meters) from the north. On February 4, they left their camp by a small lake just north of the mountain, and proceeded to ski up the valley and moraines to gain its west ridge above the Epaulette Col. When the group reached the highest skiable point, six of its members, including the leader, turned back because of bad visibility, strong wind, and cold, while the other four took one rope, removed their skis, and climbed up steep snow to the ridge.

At that point Hans, who was carrying the rope, decided to stop and find shelter. The remaining three continued up the ridge toward the summit, spaced about 50 meters apart. When Frank, who was second, reached the base of the steep final slope, he could no longer see Russ ahead of him. Looking around, he spotted a meter wide hole in the show a short distance back. Russ had fallen into some kind of crevasse. Frank shouted for him, and got a response from the depths. When the third man, Peter, arrived, he belayed Frank on slings to the edge of the crevasse to help Russ climb out. Russ had a deep gash over his eyebrow from smashing into the far side of the hole as he fell in, and blood was flowing from it, over his face, beard, and wind suit.

Frank and Pete patched him up, and then they all returned to camp for hot tea, a cleanup, and a better bandaging job before the entire group skied out.

Analysis
The climbers feel there was no indication of any hazard, as they had been simply moving along a mixed snow and rock ridge, "as we have all scrambled over numerous times before without a second thought" and "There is nothing in this spot which would make a climber want to rope up." Perhaps in good weather conditions a better overall view of the surroundings would have given them some indication. But in the existing bad conditions, it would have been prudent to take extra precautions, especially traveling over snow on a high mountain which has a permanent ice cap. (Source: Orvel Miskiw, ACC Calgary Section)

STRANDED ON WATERFALL ICE
British Columbia, Coast Mountains, Pemeberton Area
On December 22, 1990, three ice climbers were on a waterfall at Soo Bluffs. The leader, N.Z. (29), got to within about eight meters of the top of the pitch, and then was unable to continue or place a belay, partly due to thin ice. He dropped the rope so that his two companions could climb around the pitch and reach him from above, but they did not succeed and so went for help. The temperature was about -15C.

About 1600 the RCMP, and then the Whistler SAR, were contacted. As no local helicopter qualified for night operation was available, the Armed Forces in Comox was notified. A Labrador helicopter and a Buffalo aircraft were dispatched to the scene. By the light of flares dropped from the Buffalo, the Labrador retrieved the stranded climber about midnight; he was taken to a Whistler clinic and kept overnight to have his toes treated for frostbite. (Source: Ian Kay, Vancouver)

Analysis
At best, the leader may have just been a victim of bad luck, avoidable only by staying home that day. At worst, he misjudged the difficulty of the climb and the quality of the ice, versus his ability. At every level of ability, it is safest to overestimate the challenge. (Source: Orvel Miskiw, ACC Calgary Section)

SCALDED BY BOILING WATER
British Columbia, Purcell Mountains, Bugaboo Group
On August 4, 1990, C.F. and B.F. were cooking in camp above Conrad Kain Hut when a pot of boiling water was knocked off a Svea stove and over the boots of C.F. Second-degree burns to both ankles resulted. The victim was evacuated from the hut by helicopter. (Source: Fred Stanley, Lee Tibbert)

Analysis
Although this accident did not involve climbing, it is included because mountaineers far from help are occasionally left injured or without shelter because of a mishap with a stove. (Source: Orvel Miskiw, AAC Calgary Section)

FALL ON ROCK, NO "SPOTTING" PROTECTION
British Columbia, Purcell Mountains, Vowell Group

A large group from the ACC General Mountaineering Camp below the Vowell Glacier were bouldering at Tamarack Glen above the north margin of the glacier on July 27, 1990, when one of them, J.D., lost her balance on a ledge, and dropped to the ground about three meters below, doing "two spectacular leaps" on the way and striking her heels three times in all. She then had difficulty walking, because of pain.

The subject's feet were immersed in cold water to reduce swelling, and the group then helped her to get down the exposed moraine to the Vowell Glacier and about one kilometer back to the camp. She suffered a chipped metatarsal bone in her left foot.

Analysis
The group leader had clearly advised everyone to stay low on the rocks and to have a "spotter" for protection. The subject did not take the advice seriously enough—all too easy to do in pleasant surroundings. (Source: Fred Stanley, Lee Tibbert)

FALL ON SNOW/ICE, UNROPED
British Columbia, Purcell Mountains, Vowell Group

On August 1, 1990, two climbers were descending snow and ice unroped, about 50 meters below the summit of Peak 9250 (north of Little Howser) when one of them slipped on loose rock under his crampon, and tumbled about ten meters, badly injuring his left ankle.

His partner descended alone until able to get the attention of an Alpine Club of Canada party crossing the Vowell Glacier below. While the ACC General Mountaineering Camp was being notified, two persons lowered the victim several pitches down steep snow and made him as comfortable as possible on the glacier.

A backup ACC party arrived at 2130, too late for helicopter evacuation, but set up a camp and took over care of the victim, while the first party returned to the G.M. camp.

The victim and his partner were evacuated by helicopter at first light the next morning. The injury was a fracture of the left ankle.

Analysis
The victim was experienced, but one rescuer was quite emphatic that he would not have undertaken to descend the slope on which the accident happened. Perhaps the style of descent was inappropriate. In any case, a rope is often useful in such situations. (Source: Fred Stanley, Lee Tibbert)

SLIP ON LOOSE ROCK, UNROPED
British Columbia, Rocky Mountains, Mount Assiniboine

In August, 1990, two climbers were descending the northeast ridge of Mount Assiniboine after a successful ascent. Two rappels down the ridge, one of them (54) was traversing unroped toward another rappel anchor when he slipped on loose rock and fell 700 meters to his death. His partner descended alone until he could attract the attention of others, who sent for help and came to his assistance.

Analysis
Climbing Mount Assiniboine had been the victim's ambition for some time. He had worked hard to become prepared and fit, and intended to retire from climbing after this ascent. His slip was great caution. (Source: T. Auger, Warden Service, Banff National Park)

FALL ON SNOW, ROPED BUT NOT BELAYED, INEXPERIENCE
British Columbia, Rocky Mountains, Mount Robson
At approximately 1230 on August 21, 1990, Kofler and Herbst (30) were descending from the summit of Mount Robson. Herbst fell and slid down the southwest side of the ridge they were on, pulling Kofler off. Both fell approximately 75 meters, flying over a crevasse and hitting the bottom edge, which stopped them. Kofler sustained a broken ankle, Herbst had facial cuts and a black eye. Kofler lost his ice ax, and Herbst lost one crampon.

A party of two climbers, Guerra and Glick, who were ascending the summit ridge, met another party, Stefanoff and Warner, who were descending and heard cries for help from Kofler and Herbst, above. Guerra and Glick assisted the injured climbers to a bivy site in a bergschrund at the top of the Kain Face, southeast ridge. Stefanoff and Warner descended to get help.

Two mountain guides, Blanchard and Kirwin, who were camped at the base of the Kain Face with three clients, ascended to the bivy site with supplies after hearing about the accident from Stefanoff and Warner. The guides then descended to their clients while the remaining four climbers spent the night at the bivy.

Jasper National Park Warden Service received information about the accident late on the day it occurred, and dispatched a helicopter and rescue team the following morning, August 22. The same morning Glick and Guerra attempted to descent but were turned back by heavy snow and whiteout conditions, as a major storm had moved in overnight.

Bad weather made it impossible for the helicopter to reach the injured party; however, at 1610, a small window opened up at 3200 meters below the injured party. At 2000, the helicopter was able to drop off a radio at Blanchard and Kirwin's camp at the bottom of the Kain Face (on the side opposite from Little Robson). Shortly after that, they ascended the Kain Face, arriving at the injured party's bivy site at 2230. The decision was made to move them down the Kain Face immediately because the forecast was for the weather to deteriorate further. They reached the lower camp four hours later, at 0230, August 23.

At 1340 on August 23, the helicopter picked up the injured climbers at the camping area below the Kain Face.

Analysis
Aside from the fall, this accident resulted primarily from inexperience. Kofler and Herbst had taken only one climbing school together. They were not prepared either in ability or equipment for a climb as rigorous as Mount Robson. Proper belay techniques on steep terrain and the ability to self-arrest are essential skills for such a climb. A severe storm that suddenly struck Mount Robson complicated the rescue. It was very fortunate that Kofler and Herbst encountered experienced mountaineers to assist them in their predicament. (Source: Rick Ralf, Canadian Parks Service, Jasper)

CORRECTIONS—ANAM, 1990

Page 10, near the bottom of the page: The mountain referred to is Mount Niblock, not "Nublock" as stated.

Page 12, near the middle of the page: The glacier referred to is the Mangin, not "Magin" as stated.

Page 17: The "rocks" used here were in fact manufactured protection, though the term was not capitalized. "Rock" is a trade name of Wild Country U.K., Ltd., for a range of curved and tapered wired chocks. They quickly became very popular, at least across Canada and the United States, after appearing in 1982, are available in several countries, and are still widely used.

UNITED STATES

CORNICE COLLAPSE
Alaska, Mount Deception

On April 2, 1990, Jim Bouchard (34) and Gary Donofrio (27) departed the Parks Highway for their approach to climb Mount Deception at 3600 meters. On April 7, they made it to their 1730 meter basecamp on the Eldridge Glacier. Over the 8th, they ascended the southeast spur to 2280 meters, where they built a snow cave. Departing early the next morning, they continued up the ridge. Around noon they had stopped for a short break. At 1230, Donofrio continued to lead out along the corniced ridge. Bouchard was quickly putting items back into his pack, before giving Donofrio a belay, when a large section of corniced ridge collapsed, carrying Donofrio down a 75 degree slope. The fracture line was within 60 centimeters of Bouchard. He lost his ice ax with the cornice. Donofrio had walked out about 12 meters attempting to stay in the softer snow noticing the lip consisted of much firmer snow. Bouchard witnessed the fall and immediately realized his only option was to jump off the opposite side of the ridge since he was tied into the 50 meter rope. Bouchard leaped off attempting to make as much distance down the 60 degree slope as possible. Within ten meters he felt the force from Donofrio which began to drag him back up the slope. Bouchard fought this reverse pull by digging in his crampons and hands on the icy slope. Donofrio finally came to a stop about 45 meters down the face. He did not lose consciousness, but went into severe shock from internal injuries. Bouchard belay hoisted Donofrio back to the ridge crest where it was apparent they had to quickly descend their ascent route. Over the next ten hours, Bouchard belayed Donofrio back to their basecamp. Donofrio was able to descend unassisted but experienced severe chest and back pain. The next morning, Bouchard departed for the road at 0700, realizing Donofrio could not continue in his present condition. At 1430, he arrived at Chulitna River Lodge where he called Denali National Park headquarters for assistance. At 1445, the Talkeetna Ranger station received Bouchard's request where, at 1500, the Rescue Coordination Center was contacted. Army CH47 helicopters had been practicing with the Talkeetna mountaineering staff this same day and were deployed to the scene along with four Mountaineering Rangers. Bouchard was picked up from the lodge at 1647, arriving 20 minutes later at their basecamp. Donofrio was transported by litter to the helicopter and then flown to Humana Hospital in Anchorage. (Source: Roger Robinson, Mountaineering Ranger, Denali National Park)

FALL ON SNOW, PLACED NO PROTECTION, EXPOSURE
Alaska, Mount McKinley

On May 16, 1990, the three member "Washington Square" party of Mary Koshuta, Michael Koshuta (33) and Stuart Jones (29) flew into the 2200 meter basecamp on

Mount McKinley. Their objective was first to acclimatize on the West Buttress, then Mr. Koshuta and Jones would ascend the Cassin Ridge. While they were at the Kahiltna basecamp, they had the opportunity to talk with Michael Covington, mountain guide and head of the Guide Service Fantasy Ridge. Covington had just returned from guiding on the Cassin and gave the pair additional information about the route. Covington had guided Mr. Koshuta on several trips in the past, including Mount Huntington, where Jones was also a client. Covington's group of six was unable to traverse over the summit because of severe weather, so they made a traverse at the 5000 meter level, descending off the Cassin and traversing over 40 pitches to the West Rib. He felt the traverse would not be a safe escape off the Cassin if one were in trouble. It should only be undertaken in good weather. Covington went over this information with Koshuta and Jones.

By May 21, the three had reached 3350 meters, where they spent several days acclimatizing. By the 24th they had returned to Kahiltna basecamp. Mary Koshuta returned to Talkeetna, and Mr. Koshuta and Jones began their approach to the Cassin. On the 25th, Koshuta and Jones went up the Northeast Fork with approximately twelve days of food. On the 30th, the "Idaho Centennial," a team of three, met up with Koshuta and Jones on the Cassin Ledge at 1030. Koshuta and Jones were packing up their camp. The two teams had about a two hour overlap. After Koshuta and Jones had departed, another group of two, Kevin Steele and Rob Raker of the "Black Diamond" team, arrived on the Cassin Ledge. On the 31st, the Black Diamond and Idaho Centennial teams moved up to 4300 meters. On June 1, the two teams rested in good weather at this location where they observed Koshuta and Jones ascending the route between 4575 meters and 4785 meters. On June 2, the Black Diamond and Idaho teams ascended to 4550 meters, stopping here due to light snow and spindrift avalanches. Later that evening, Tony Moats and Chris Whittaker, "New Skids," arrived at this level. All three teams departed the next day and ascended to 4800 meters. Late that evening Moats and Whittaker saw someone dressed in red ascending the second rock band at 4900 meters. Later at midnight, Flanagen saw someone at 4970 meters. On June 4, all three teams departed the 4785 meter camp and ascended to 5330 meters. As they climbed past the last technical difficulty, they observed a very recent tent platform dug out in the last day, indicating very recent usage. Over the next two days a cold storm struck the mountain with winds blowing a steady 30-80 kph and gusts to 100 kph. On the 7th, all seven continued higher with New Skids and Idaho ascending to 5500 meters and the Black Diamond pair ascending to 6125 meters. On the 8th, the winds continued again.

The New Skids went to the summit and then down the West Buttress to 4320 meters. Black Diamond went to the summit and down to 5950 meters on the West Buttress. On the 9th, the Idaho team made the summit and descended to 4320 meters on the West Buttress. All three teams observed no further sign of Koshuta and Jones.

On June 10, the Talkeetna Ranger Station began to make inquiries into the status of the Washington Square team since they were two days overdue. On the 11th, Mary Koshuta provided additional information which made it possible to check the Washington Square's caches left on the West Buttress. The Idaho team uncovered the cache at 3350 meters where it had not been disturbed. It was apparent an air search was needed. Extensive aerial flights began with both fixed with aircraft and Army helicopters. (The Army was available because of a rescue taking place on the West Buttress.) Search efforts continued until the bodies of Koshuta and Jones were spotted on the 12th at 4800 meters, four-fifths of the distance between the Cassin and West Rib. It appeared they had fallen roped together. They were buried at their location because of the difficulty a ground evacuation would encounter. (Source: Roger Robinson, Mountaineering Ranger, Denali National Park)

Analysis
Koshuta and Jones attempted the traverse from the Cassin Ridge to the West Rib some time between June 5 and June 7. It is uncertain whether they were belaying, but it appears they were not when the fall occurred. Jones was obviously leading and dressed lightly while Koshuta was dressed much warmer. Due to this clothing difference, they probably had belayed sections of the traverse. If they had placed protection, their fall may have been stopped.

It will remain unknown what prompted the two to attempt the traverse, but a reasonable guess would suggest they needed off the Cassin because of the shortage in food and fuel and the possibility the severe weather on the 5th and 6th had damaged their tent. There are many other altitude related possibilities. In any case, they attempted the traverse.

They had been cautioned about the difficulties in attempting the traverse and about it not being a safe route for an escape off the Cassin. In light of this warning and the fact that there were seven strong climbers just 250 meters below them, a descent of the Cassin would have been the safest option. (Source: Roger Robinson, Mountaineering Ranger, Denali National Park)

CEREBRAL EDEMA, PARTY SEPARATED, INEXPERIENCE
Alaska, Mount McKinley
On May 27, 1990, a three member Sophia University expedition flew onto the Southeast Fork of the Kahiltna Glacier of Mount McKinley to climb the West Buttress. The three inexperienced climbers reached the 5250 meter camp on June 11. Atuhiro Onodera (23) had a headache and no appetite upon arrival.

On June 14, the three went toward the summit, but at 5800 meters, Onodera was unable to continue due to a loss of balance, headache, and shortness of breath. He was left and his partners continued. While descending, a solo American came across Onodera and had to assist him back to 5250 meters due to his ataxia.

Onodera had no memory about the summit attempt, slept for most of the next two days, ate and drank very little, and had difficulty in walking.

By the afternoon of the 16th, the Japanese Wind Expedition examined Onodera and told the Sophia expedition they had to descend immediately. Since Onodera was having difficulty in walking, he was put on oxygen and taken from the NPS rescue cache and helped down the Rescue Gully to the NPS 4300 meter camp.

At 0200 on June 17, Onodera was examined by Ranger Scott Gill. Onodera was unable to perform the heel to toe test without falling down. He was put on oxygen for 45 minutes and seemed to improve immensely. After an evening at the NPS camp, he was able to descend under his own power and flown out from basecamp. (Source: Scott Gill, Mountaineering Ranger, Denali National Park)

HAPE, DESIRE TO DO WELL
Alaska, Mount McKinley
Craig Scott (30) was a member of a RMI expedition to climb the West Buttress route on Mount McKinley. The expedition flew onto the Kahiltna Glacier on June 2, 1990. Scott was a triathlete and was doing very well throughout the climb. On June 7, the expedition reached the 4260 meter camp. Scott was starting to feel the altitude and had a difficult time sleeping and breathing that evening. He did not tell any of the guides of his condition until late morning on the 8th.

At 1300 Scott was helped up, as he was unable to walk unassisted, to the NPS camp. Upon examination by Dr. Steve Gipe, Scott was found to have coarse rales on both sides of his lungs. Gipe classified Scott as having severe pulmonary edema and put him on oxygen.

RMI started organizing to take Scott down the mountain immediately. Scott responded to oxygen and felt much better. After four hours, Scott was put on a portable "E" oxygen bottle with a cannula in his mouth and was able to descend under his own power. The evacuation got Scott down to 2450 meters that night. He improved rapidly with descent. (Source: Scott Gill, Mountaineering Ranger, Denali National Park)

Analysis
The importance of being "up front" with your medical condition in regard to altitude cannot be overemphasized. Scott could have died if he had kept his symptoms from the guides much longer. The oxygen enabled Scott to descend under his own power. RMI did an excellent job getting Scott down once the problem was diagnosed. (Source: Scott Gill, Mountaineering Ranger, Denali National Park)

FALL ON SNOW, AVALANCHE, INADEQUATE EQUIPMENT
Alaska, Bold Peak
On June 3, 1990, two experienced Alaskan mountaineers set out to climb Bold Peak (2286 meters) located in the Eklutna Lake area of the Chugach Mountains. They planned the ascent to take two days, the first for the approach and the second for ascent, descent, and departure. The approach, from 265 meters, involved almost ten kilometers via mountain bike over unimproved dirt road followed by several kilometers on foot to treeline and then over tundra, gradually climbing to the base of the north-west face of Bold Peak. Here the climbers, Tim Doyle (38) and Mark Norquist (34), set up their base camp at the 1200 meter level.

They left their base camp at 0700, June 4. Carrying what Doyle describes as "only the bare essentials of climbing," they crossed a small glacier to reach the base of some large snowfields dominating the northwest face. As they ascended steep slopes, the climbers crossed many snow trenches left by small avalanches and wet snow slides. They gained the northeast ridge at 1400, and reached the summit an hour later. After resting on the summit, Doyle and Norquist began retracing their earlier route on descent.

By the time they reached the face, the snow had softened in direct afternoon sun. The soft, wet snow formed icy balls under their crampons as they crossed the open snowfield. The face was now striped with many slide paths. Before reaching his intended glissade route, Doyle fell and was instantly swept head first into a large trough.

Trapped in the trough, there was no escape. Doyle recalls, "My self-arrest wouldn't hold. There was no hope of control. The noise level rose as I gathered momentum. There was no air to breathe."

He finally rolled to a stop after sliding about 600 vertical meters. The wet avalanche had deposited him on the surface of the snowfield. Norquist found Doyle 20 minutes later, sitting upright in avalanche debris. It appeared that Doyle had suffered a broken ankle and contusions covering his face and head. After deciding that Doyle's condition was somewhat stable, Norquist left the accident site to retrieve overnight gear from base camp. Doyle remained at 1500 meters dressed in all their excess clothing and lying on the insulation of a rope, pack, and some webbing. Doyle, immobilized by his injuries, would need a comfortable bivouac, while Norquist went for help.

Approximately 15 minutes after they parted, another avalanche struck Doyle, carrying him further down the slope and leaving him nearly buried. The second slide was larger than the first, and deposited him upside down with only one foot sticking out of the snow. Over an hour would pass before his release.

Norquist returned to what he thought was the original accident site, but could find no trace of Doyle. He climbed at least 150 vertical meters higher in search of his partner, and then descended with a full view of the snowfield. He found Doyle's exposed leg wiggling among the icy blocks of the second avalanche. The extrication took at least 20 minutes. The snow had set hard and the only tools Norquist had were his ice ax and hands, their only shovel having been lost earlier.

Norquist moved his partner to a safer bivouac spot, placed Doyle in a sleeping bag and attempted to stabilize his condition before leaving for help at 2030. He then ran down past the place where he and Doyle had hidden and double locked their bikes. He didn't stop there because, although he had remembered Doyle's key, he had accidentally discarded his own while changing clothes to run for help. He ran the ten kilometers to the parking lot and drove to the nearby Eklutna Ranger Station. The Alaska State Troopers received his call on 0200 on June 4.

The Troopers initiated an emergency callout to the Alaska Mountain Rescue Group (AMRG). By 0400, a Bell 206 helicopter from the State Department of Forestry and several members of the AMRG team had arrived at the ranger station. Seven rescuers were flown to the accident site to aid the evacuation.

Tim Doyle was in good spirits despite spending a long, pain-filled night on the snow. He was treated for a broken ankle, dehydration and possible back injuries before being placed in a litter for transport. A helicopter landing zone had to be shoveled out of the avalanche debris. The litter was placed crosswise in the back half of the helicopter from which the back seats and door had been removed. An attendant rode back with the patient, whose feet hung out of the helicopter.

Doyle was transferred to a waiting ambulance at the Eklutna Ranger Station at 0530. His actual injuries included: broken right tibia and fibula, right shoulder dislocation, dislocation of both hips, broken fingers and toes, and major contusions of his head, face and hands. (Source: To prepare this report, I interviewed Tom Doyle and Mark Norquist twice each and read all of their published accounts. Steve Brown, Vice-Chairperson— Alaska Mountain Rescue Group)

Analysis

The climbers were off to a leisurely, if not late, start at 0700. This resulted in their late afternoon descent with wet snow conditions. In June, the northwest face receives both morning and afternoon sun. Although both were aware of the unstable conditions and recent slide activity, they chose to continue down the open face. Gambling with this route, rather than attempting another more stable, protected one (the Northeast Ridge), set the stage for the accidents which followed.

Although both climbers now recall the slope on the ascent as having been solid and frozen, their summit register entry complains of sloppy snow. The freezing level was high at the time of the accident, probably staying above 2500 meters during what passes for night in the Chugach in early June.

After Doyle's first fall, Norquist attempted to move him to safety, but did not clear him completely from the many slide paths. Neither climber carried an avalanche transceiver and they had only one shovel. They were not equipped for avalanche conditions. Doyle survived burial in the second avalanche through luck, fortitude and the perseverance of his partner.

Norquist made two difficult decisions, concluding that he must leave Doyle alone and injured on the snowfields of Bold Peak. He had to have great willpower to complete the 19 hours of strenuous physical and emotional activity required to save Doyle and get help for the evacuation. The rescue effort by the Alaska Mountain Rescue Group, coordinated with the Alaska State Troopers, was simplified by Doyle's miraculously stable condition. From the time Norquist first contacted the Troopers, it took less than four hours to complete the evacuation. (Source: Steve Brown and Ken Zafren, M.D., Alaska Mountain Rescue Group)

HAPE, FROSTBITE, PARTY SEPARATED, INEXPERIENCE, WEATHER
Alaska, Mount McKinley

On June 10, 1990, at the top of the West Rib (5975 meters) on Mount McKinley, Miroaki Ito (38) died from pulmonary edema. Ito had been left here, since he was feeling poorly, while the other six members of the KTK expedition went for the summit. Upon descent from the summit, two members got lost in poor visibility and descended the popular West Buttress route to the NPS 4260 meter camp. The others remained at the 5975 meter camp in extreme wind and cold, with very little gear, in hopes of locating their two countrymen.

By morning on June 10, Ito was near death and three others were severely frostbitten. A ground team was organized along with air support to help rescue the KTK expedition. By late afternoon Ito had died, and the frostbitten members of the KTK expedition were being evacuated to the 4260 meter camp where their extremities were rewarmed.

On June 11, Kiyoteru Hashimoto (25), Shin Kashu (41), and Takashi Nishikawa (36) were air lifted by Army CH-47 Chinook helicopter from the NPS camp, as they were unable to walk due to the severity of their frostbite. (Source: Scott Gill, Mountaineering Ranger, Denali National Park)

Analysis

The team set out on an apparently good day from 5500 meters and fixed rope to 5950 meters. Mr. Ito developed cough, a staggering walk and shortness of breath, which are obvious signs of severe altitude illness. One member of his group was an experienced Himalayan climber and it is hard to understand how he did not recognize the seriousness of Ito's condition. At that point, descent would have been very easy on fixed lines and with good weather, and since they were only 450 vertical meters above their camp, it would have been a very rapid trip back to their high camp.

The decision to leave him because he was not feeling well and to continue on up to the summit is probably the single greatest cause of altitude deaths on mountaineering expeditions. A victim of altitude illness who cannot walk a straight line or appears to have pulmonary edema must never be left alone. The appropriate action is to descend immediately, and not to have the victim descend by himself.

The decision to not turn around on the ascent, and to bivouac at 5950 meters with an obviously very ill man may have been due, in part, to hypoxia. The fact that they couldn't find the trail down the next day, nor drag him down across easy terrain because they were in such poor condition, points to incapacitation due to altitude, exhaustion and other environmental conditions.

In summary, this case illustrates the classic causes of death due to altitude illness: (1) lack of recognition that a person is seriously ill; (2) leaving a sick person behind while the rest of the group continues on; and (3) the deteriorating condition of an entire group of climbers under extreme conditions. (Source: Dr. Peter H. Hackett)

FALL ON SNOW, INEXPERIENCE
Alaska, Eklutna Glacier

On July 13, five climbers were injured, one critically, in a 60 meter fall on Eklutna Glacier. The climbers, part of an 18-member international expedition, tumbled down the glacier on Saturday afternoon and were stranded until early Sunday morning. They were airlifted to Providence Hospital.

One of the five, 24-year old Jackie Feaver of England, was comatose and listed in critical condition with serious head injuries Sunday night.

Ying Ju Loi of Malaysia and Nicky Kime of England, both 25, were in satisfactory condition at Providence. Two other climbers, Australian Helen Philips (26) and Gavin Burke (23) of England, were treated an released from the hospital Sunday.

The five climbers were roped together and traversing a snow slide when one lost footing and fell, dragging the others about 60 meters down the glacier.

Two other climbers, Iain Bernsten and Vincent Diamond, left the scene about two hours later and hiked about 24 km to a park service cabin at Eklutna Lake for help.

Wolgemuth said a state trooper helicopter and a hospital helicopter flew to the glacier about 0230 on Sunday; the helicopters arrived at Providence with the climbers about 0430. (Source: Anchorage Daily News, July 15, 1990)

Analysis

Mercer, a public relations specialist for Operation Raleigh, the London-based outfit that sponsored the expedition, said they were in good spirits. "They were just coming off the glacier," Mercer said. "One slipped, and the others went with them.

"They all had the correct equipment, helmets and crampons and so on, and each group has a medic and a qualified instructor with them. All the basic precautions were taken."

Mercer said Operation Raleigh is "a youth development program out of London" that takes young people between the ages of 17 and 25 on expeditions around the world. The program combines adventure and conservation work for its clients, who "pay their own way," she said. (Source: Anchorage Daily News, July 15, 1990)

FALL ON SNOW, NOT WEARING CRAMPONS
California, Mount Shasta
On June 11, 1989, Richard Ferrell (45) and his brother Brett Ferrell (31) were climbing on Sergeants Ridge on Mount Shasta. They had ice axes and were carrying (but not wearing) crampons. Richard Ferrell either slipped or was knocked down by falling debris. He slid/tumbled about 300 meters to a point above the old ski bowl at 2800 meters, suffering fatal head trauma. (Source: Tom Grossman, Bay Area Mountain Rescue Unit)

FALLING ROCK, WEATHER, EXCEEDING ABILITIES
California, Mount Shasta
In early January, Lorca Rossman (19), Roman Hruska (19), and Nic Rhind (23) were turned back from their summit attempt due to high winds which were blowing rocks down from the ridges above Avalanche Gulch. They were near the 3975 meter level when they began to descend the right side of Avalanche Gulch next to the "Heart." Seasonal snowfall below normal levels had left the ridges bare, and a constant barrage of rocks came down around us. Nic Rhind chose a steeper but less exposed route of descent to avoid the rocks. Lorca Rossman chose to glissade as rapidly as possible to below the fall-zone, to reduce his exposure time. Fifteen minutes later, Lorca and Nic met near 3350 meters, and agreed that Nic would wait for Roman Hruska, who was descending slowly in the main fall-zone, while Lorca continued down to 3000 meters to break camp. Shortly after dark, Nic and Roman arrived at camp. Roman's balaclava was soaked with blood from a blow by a 30 cm falling rock. He complained of point tenderness and a generalized throbbing headache, but denied loss of consciousness or symptoms of C-spine injury. Aside from slight ataxia possibly stemming from exhaustion and mild hypothermia (temperature was -18 degrees C, wind 30 knots gusting to 70+), he showed no impairment of functioning, and we were able to hike him out to the road at 2100 meters by 0100. E.R. evaluation revealed a 10 cm laceration without fracture or complications. (Source: Lorca Rossman)

Analysis
The combination of bare ridges and high winds created an objective hazard that was clearly visible. The accident might have been prevented by more careful attention on the victim's part to a descent strategy that minimized exposure, or by better communication about appropriate descent strategies. None of us wore hard hats, believing that winter snow would preclude rock-fall danger. More careful attention to the actual conditions would have been appropriate. (Source: Lorca Rossman)

PROTECTION PULLED OUT, FALL ON ROCK
California, Owens Gorge
On June 17 a friend, Courtney Smith (?), fell while climbing in Owens Gorge in eastern California. The climb he was on started from a three meter high ledge, ascending about five meters to the first bolt and then on up. He got on the ledge, didn't like the distance to the first bolt, and protected with a Friend in a crack about three meters to the side of his climb. He started to downclimb without asking for slack from his belayer, weighting the rope somewhat. The Friend popped out of the crack, and he fell over a meter to the ledge, and then another three or four meters to the ground.

The ledge tumbled him backwards in the fall; he landed on his side and head, shattering his jaw and breaking his wrist. He went for an ambulance; luckily, the walk-in was short and he didn't need a stretcher. (Source: Doug Mellinger)

FALL ON ROCK, CLIMBING UNROPED, PLACED NO PROTECTION
California, Yosemite Valley

On July 10, while free soloing Comfortably Numb, a 5.10 climb on Cottage Dome, Susan Green (21) fell about 15-24 meters, landing upright on both feet. He then slid an additional 20 meters down a slab, sliding over one additional three meter drop. Nearby climbers hiked out and reported the accident to Tuolomne Rangers via the Mountaineering School director.

A first response NPS team of three plus the reporting party hiked to the accident scene with medical and helicopter evacuation equipment. The NPS helicopter was requested. Greer was stabilized utilizing a KED, air splits, and secured in a litter. An IV was established, and oxygen therapy was initiated. An additional ground evacuation team was hiked into the scene in the event the helicopter was unavailable. Helicopter 51 flew to the scene and was unable to land. Greer was short hauled from the scene to a nearby LZ, where he was loaded into the helicopter and transported to the Yosemite Medical Clinic. He was later evacuated to Memorial North Hospital via Mediflight. Subsequent follow-up with the Yosemite Medical Clinic showed Greer to have bilateral fractures of the tibia and fibula. (Source: James Tucker, Ranger, Yosemite Valley National Park)

FALL ON ROCK, CLIMBING UNROPED, NO HARD HAT, INTOXICATED
California, Yosemite Valley

Around 1830 on July 15, Troy Johnson (22) met with Bill Russell. Russell stated Johnson at that particular time was intoxicated, yet expressed his desire to perform a solo over the Church Bowl. According to Russell, Johnson was climbing a route currently known as "Revised," rated at 10(a). No ropes or protection was utilized. Approximately two to three meters up, Russell heard Johnson yell, "Oh, shit!" and then heard Johnson's body hit the ground. When he approached Johnson on the ground to offer assistance, he observed no active respirations. He initiated artificial respirations and Johnson began to breath spontaneously. Significant amounts of hemorrhaging was observed from the back of his head. At that time Russell went for help. Johnson was taken to the clinic, and then, after stabilization, was taken to a hospital. Initial prognosis was not favorable, but he has made nearly a full recovery. (Source: Thomas Wilson, Ranger, Yosemite National Park)

Analysis

We were informed that Johnson had been reportedly consuming alcoholic beverages throughout the day. At least eight 354 ml. cans of Old English 800 Malt Liquor have been traced to have been consumed by Johnson on that day with the possibility of additional consumption prior to those accounted. The majority of these beverages were purchased by Johnson at the Deli. At approximately 1810, Johnson was reported to be under the influence by an off duty NPS employee. During a brief conversation,

Johnson was quoted to have said, "Old English is courage in a can." (Source: Thomas Wilson, Ranger, Yosemite National Park)

FALL ON ROCK, CLIMBING UNROPED, INADEQUATE FOOTWEAR
California, Yosemite Valley

On July 18, Amy Khoo (19), Matthew Enu (24) and a newly met climbing partner, Joey Chiarucci (26) were using technical climbing equipment to climb the lower Yosemite Falls waterfall route, just to the east of lower Yosemite Falls. They completed this climb safely, and then secured their climbing gear in their backpacks. They remained at the top of the lower falls for a few hours, swimming in the pool there.

They then attempted to descend from the area by first climbing to the top of a granite bench by which they then were going to walk off from the climb, going to the east across Sunnyside bench. At this point they were not wearing their climbing boots. In fact, Amy Khoo was wearing Birkenstock sandals. As Khoo attempted to climb to the top of the bench, she lost her footing and fell about eight meters down a moderate angle slope. She was injured, knocking out several teeth, possibly fracturing her left femur, and sustaining multiple areas of significant abrasions to her arms and legs. Matthew rappelled down to her, determined that she needed medical attention and a technical evacuation, and sent Joey Chiarucci down to the NPS Maintenance Yard where he contacted Ranger Cameron Jacobi at 1910. I organized an immediate response, sending a blitz team headed by John Dill up Sunnyside Bench with initial medical and technical gear. A follow-up team, headed by Jacobi then geared up and followed Dill a half hour later. Due to darkness, Khoo was not evacuated by helicopter. Litter evacuation was completed by 0100 on July 19. (Source: James Tucker, Ranger, Yosemite National Park.)

FALL ON ICE, PLACED NO PROTECTION
California, Mount Shasta

In July, a party of four climbers attempted the Hotlum Glacier route on Mount Shasta. Parts of this route are covered in hard ice on which self-arrest is difficult. The climbers traveled in two two-man roped teams, and used ice axes and crampons. While traveling over a section of hard ice, one member of rope team #1 fell and took his rope-mate with him. Both suffered injuries to the lower legs from crampon points. Later, one member of rope team #2 fell and slid, pulling his rope-mate after him. During their 300 meter slide, one of the victims hooked a crampon point on the ice, injuring his ankle and causing him to tumble. The pair stopped around 3200 meters by dragging their knees and elbows against the ice. The injured victim was unable to travel and spent the night alone on the glacier, suffering frostbite to the injured foot. He was evacuated by Siskiyou County SAR the following morning. (Source: Tom Grossman, Bay Area Mountain Rescue Unit)

Analysis

The ice on the Hotlum Glacier is often hard enough to make self-arrest extremely difficult; this means that simultaneous roped travel does not significantly increase (and in fact may decrease) the safety of the climbing party. In each of these two incidents, the main effect of the rope was to convert a one-person accident into a two-person accident.

The common technique of simultaneous roped travel is of great value when traveling over crevassed glaciers where self-arrest is reliable. However, climbers traveling over snow or ice should keep in mind that they have many alternatives, and the "standard" technique of simultaneous roped travel may not be the best under all circumstances. Depending on conditions and skill level, climbers can (besides doing simultaneous roped climbing: (1) climb unroped, (2) use a static belay, (3) use a running belay or (4) change their plans! (Source: Tom Grossman, Bay Area Mountain Rescue Unit)

FALL ON ROCK, INADEQUATE PROTECTION, EXCEEDING ABILITIES
California, Yosemite Valley

On August 2, about noon, Matthew Tomlinson (28) fell while lead climbing Keystone Corner (5.8) at Five and Dime Cliff. He was flown by Helicopter 51 from the scene to the Yosemite Medical Clinic where he was pronounced dead at 1600.

An interview with his climbing partner, Denise Brown (32), revealed the following.

Brown and Tomlinson both finished their shifts at The Loft restaurant on August 1 at 2330 and went together in Brown's car to her residence. They discussed the climb they were to do the next day and worked on some new climbing hardware of Tomlinson's (putting tape on carabiners and cord on a crack cleaner, etc.). Brown said that she drank about 2 1/2 beers that night, and that Tomlinson drank one wine cooler, which Brown said was "not much" for him.

He and Brown arose about 0900 on the second. They spent time around the trailer, and left for the Five and Dime Cliff at 1100 in Brown's car. In the car, Brown and Tomlinson discussed the particulars of the climb, with which they were both familiar, having done it together, with Brown leading and Tomlinson following, the previous week. Brown told me that Tomlinson insisted on leading the climb on that day, and that it was his first lead. She said that she tried twice to talk him out of leading it, but that he strongly insisted. She said, "He was gung-ho on doing it."

They parked their car and walked down to the climb. Brown set up a belay anchor, on the tree at the base of the climb, consisting of two runners and two carabiners. She said that she set up a textbook anchor, as she felt herself to be something of an instructor to Tomlinson.

At 1200, Tomlinson started up the climb, carrying gear that belonged primarily to Brown, with some of his own. Brown said that he was "practically running up" the climb, "looking casual, looking good." She said that he looked "relaxed." He placed his first piece of protection, a Friend, at the second chalkstone in the crack of Keystone Corner, as he and Brown had discussed previously. Brown told me that she told him to put in a second piece two meters above the first, by standing at the second chalkstone and placing the next piece at chest height or above, but that Tomlinson continued to climb, not placing that second piece.

Brown said that she called to him as he started to ascend, telling him again to put in a piece. She said to me, "He didn't do it. I don't understand why... he was feeling cocky, I guess."

Tomlinson continued to climb, and put in his second piece of protection about five meters above the first, at the place where climbers usually put in their third piece. The location of that piece is at the third chalkstone in the crack, where one has to stem to the left. Tomlinson had done that stem, and called to Brown that he had, in her words, a "bomber cam" at that location; in other words, that he was comfortable with that piece of protection. (The piece that he placed there was in fact a Friend, not a cam, or Camalot.)

When Tomlinson was about a meter above that second piece, he fell. Brown said that she did not actually see the fall, that, "Any time someone falls, ... I concentrate on the rope." She said that she did not know exactly how or why Tomlinson fell, but that as soon as she felt him begin to fall, she began to pull the rope through her Sticht belay plate as quickly as she could. She said that she felt him pull out his first piece of protection, at which time she realized that she could not take up the slack in the rope fast enough, and she began to pull it in hand-over-hand in a body belay, sustaining at least one rope burn on her left bicep in the process.

Tomlinson landed on a ledge below her, about three meters directly below the tree at which she had been belaying. The fall distance she estimated around ten meters. Brown went immediately to Tomlinson, and in trying to turn him over on his back, Tomlinson slid into a large crack in the ledge, with his head upside down. Brown said that because of the bleeding from Tomlinson's head, she wanted to move him, so she went around to the base of the ledge upon which he had landed and pulled him through the crack into which he had then gone, out onto a slope. It was here that she placed him head-up, on his back.

At that time, Tomlinson was apparently not breathing, and Brown cleared a large volume of blood out of his mouth by sucking it out, then gave him artificial respirations for five to 20 minutes. (She was unsure of the length of time.) He resumed breathing on his own, and Brown ran up to the road to get help. On the road she found Kurak, who with another male, a Sean, who apparently works at the Yosemite Village Store, and Brown, went back down to Tomlinson.

Brown, Kurak, and Sean were with Tomlinson when the Park Rangers arrived on the scene. (Source: John Christiansen, Park Ranger, Yosemite National Park)

Analysis
It is apparent to me that the fact that Tomlinson's uppermost piece of protection, a #1 1/2 Friend, pulling out was the major factor contributing to the severity of the injuries that he sustained. The exact cause and mechanism of the fall are impossible to determine, due to the fact that Brown did not actually see the fall. Her instinct was apparently to look away as soon as she realized that he was falling, and her experience is that belayers often get hit in the face by falling leaders, and that she focuses her attention on the rope and not the climber.

Brown apparently made every effort possible as a belayer to stop the fall, including pulling in slack on the rope hand-over-hand in a body belay when she realized that she could not take up the slack fast enough through her belay device.

Tomlinson apparently fell from approximately one meter above the piece of protection that failed; his feet were about the level of that piece. The reasons for the piece pulling out of the crack in which it had been placed, as evidenced by its presence on the rope but not in the crack when Tomlinson was found by rescuers, are difficult to determine. Possible causes include that it may have been improperly placed, either at an improper (too shallow) angle, or in a portion of the crack that was too wide, or that the angle of pull on the piece when Tomlinson fell may not have been in line with the piece. This fact is suggested by the short distance between Tomlinson at the time of the fall and the piece.

Furthermore, the piece of protection that remained in the crack, a #1/2 friend recovered by Frank Brown and given to me, shows some evidence of having borne a load: its cam-axis piece is bowed to the point where one cam rubs against the shaft of the piece. The #1 1/2 Friend that failed shows some evidence of scraping against the cams, and no other damage. The slings and carabiners attached to both of these Friends show no damage, nor do the slings and carabiners used as a belay anchor.

The Yates Swami belt worn by Tomlinson at the time of the fall shows no evidence of failure.

John Dill's impression is that there was so much slack after the Friend pulled that the belayer was powerless to stop the fall. (Source: John Christiansen and John Dill, Rangers, Yosemite National Park)

FALL ON SNOW, FAILURE TO FOLLOW ROUTE, PLACED NO PROTECTION
California, Mount Shasta

On September 2, Lawrence Macupa (38) and David Vanderryn (32) climbed the Hotlum glacier route on Mount Shasta. The "normal" descent for the Hotlum glacier route is to go down the Hotlum-Wintun ("Hottun") snowfield. They went off-route and descended a snowfield that steepens and changes into a steep chute full of blue ice. During the descent, the victims fell/slid 50+ meters through the ice chute and over a series of cliffs and ledges onto the body of the Hotlum glacier at 3700 meters. When other climbers reached the pair, one was dead and one was believed to have a faint pulse but died shortly thereafter. The victims were using ice axes and crampons at the time of their fall. (Source: Tom Grossman, Bay Area Mountain Rescue Unit)

FALL ON SNOW, UNABLE TO SELF-ARREST
California, Mount Conness

On October 7 at 1530, Deputy Randy Hysell, the SAR Coordinator for the Mono County Sheriff's Office, called me, requesting the park's assistance with a rescue. His information was second-hand at that time; he had been told only that a climber on the Conness Glacier (adjacent to the park boundary at Mount Conness) had suffered a broken leg. Hysell asked that the park helicopter, H51, assess the situation, and I accepted.

H51 located the victim at 1618. According to Jeff Panetta, the helitack person aboard, he was with two companions about two-thirds of the way up the glacier, at 3500 meters. He was conscious, appeared stable, and indicated that his right lower leg was injured. The three climbers were roped together on a slope that was less than 35 degrees but contained several crevasses.

H51 was able to land 50 meters above the party, but evacuating the victim would require hauling him over the snow up to the ship or shorthauling him directly from his location. Given the altitude, the terrain, and the late hour, Panetta felt that a hoist from a Navy UH-1N would be faster and safer than those options, so Hysell requested a ship from Naval Air Station Lemoore. While we waited for the Lemoore, H51 dropped overnight gear to the party, and Rangers Dan Horner and John Roth prepared to be dropped off at the scene with medical gear, to spend the night if necessary.

At 1300, H51 led the Lemoore helicopter, Angel 1, to the scene. At 1840 Angel 1 loaded the victim directly aboard while in a one-skid hover and returned to Toulmne meadows. He was transferred to Centinela Hospital in Mammoth by June Lake Ambulance. His partners hiked out that night, leaving the NPS survival gear at the foot of the glacier. Rangers recovered it on October 9.

The victim, Richard Hasbrook, stated to me that all members of the party had several years of mountaineering experience and were well equipped. They had climbed the glacier and a couloir above and were descending about 1300 meters when he slipped. He immediately rolled to self-arrest, but before he had slid more than a body-length, his right crampon caught. His body rotated, his foot didn't, and he suffered a spiral fracture of his right lower leg. The party splinted it with ice axes and had gotten him a rope-length or two down the glacier when we arrived. (Source: John Dill, Ranger, Yosemite National Park)

(Editor's Note: Here is a good example of (1) a climbing party prepared to take care of itself and (2) swift and efficient decision making on the part of the SAR Ranger from Yosemite.)

STRANDED, DROPPED ROPE
California, Yosemite Valley

On October 15, after completing a single pitch 5.7 route in the Church Bowl area called Uncle Fannie Hoffman, Matthew (19) lowered his partner to the ground from a ledge and accidentally dropped his only rope. Due to impending darkness, he remained at the belay ledge and sent his partner, Miller, for help.

Hoffman had seven years of mountaineering experience; however, this was only his second technical rock lead. (Source: Kelly McCloskey, Ranger, Yosemite National Park)

(Editor's Note: There have been a number of incidents like this in the past few years, so this one is included to call attention to the need for being attentive once the apparently key part of the climbing is over.)

FALL ON ICE, CLIMBING UNROPED, PARTY SEPARATED, EXPOSURE
California, Mount Shasta

On November 4 Paul Scarborough (55) and his son Dean Scarborough (23) attempted to climb the north side of Mount Shasta. They left their base camp (located at the 3050 meter level) and proceeded via the Hotlum-Bolam Route, which is considered one of the more difficult routes on the mountain. They each carried ice axe and crampons; no other climbing equipment was brought. Much of the climb was over moderately steep, very hard blue ice on which self-arrest is extremely difficult. Conditions deteriorated as a snowstorm blew in, and around the 3950 meter level the visibility was 35 meters. At this point the pair decided to separate. Dean (with his father's encouragement) was to continue to the summit, while Paul was to return to base camp. Dean summitted and returned to base camp, where he found no evidence of Paul's return. Dean hiked out to their vehicle and contacted Siskiyou County SAR. (Source: Tom Grossman, Bay Area Mountain Rescue Unit)

Analysis

Paul Scarborough's body was found on November 11 at 3350 meters by two climbers after an intensive week-long search. (It is believed that the body was buried in snow until that morning.) No ice ax was in evidence. He had sustained superficial head lacerations, and fractures to the leg, arm and ribs; the cause of death was established as hypothermia. It is speculated that he lost his footing, and tumbled/slid several hundred feet down the ice, and that his ice ax was lost during the fall. One of the victim's crampons was dislodged; it is not known if this happened before or during the fall.

It is common (especially in low snow years) for the north side of Mount Shasta to be covered in "blue ice." This blue ice is old, highly transformed snow that is clear and extremely hard and brittle. It can require a fair amount of technique to place specialized ice-climbing tools from a good stance into blue ice; in the event of a fall on this ice, self-arrest may not be possible. In such conditions, unbelayed simultaneous roped travel is not advisable. The decision whether or not to use a belay needs to be carefully considered. In the absence of a belay, traveling unroped may be preferable.

There were several accidents on Mount Shasta over the past three years. These accidents resulted in five deaths and numerous injuries, many of which go unreported. It is important that climbers recognize that ascent routes on Mount Shasta vary dramatically in difficulty, and that experience obtained on the easier routes may not be sufficient for the harder routes.

Climbers should be aware that they can obtain current information on conditions 24 hours a day by calling (916) 926-5555. (Source: Tom Grossman, Bay Area Mountain Rescue Unit)

(Editor's Note: Dennis Burge, China Lake Mountain Rescue Group, reported three accidents which occurred on Mount Whitney and North Palisade. One was a climbing accident which resulted from a neophyte losing control on a glissade. Burge made an interesting observation regarding the contributing cause: "It is interesting that two accidents occurred within four days of each other on the same slope. Climbing Mount Whitney by the trail is not mountaineering in the summer season, but in November with ice on the trail, it becomes mountaineering. That both victims had ice axes is further evidence of this. The lack of snow this November, due to our drought, caused people to think about climbing it in the late season who probably would not have otherwise tried it then. Over the years there have been many accidents on the same slope in late September and October (at least one fatal). The fact that the permit quota system for overnight climbs makes it hard to get a reservation in the summer season without planning long in advance may also be a contributory factor to these late season climbs and accidents. The quota period now ends on October 15."

The Angeles Chapter of the Sierra Club reported nine accidents for 1990, six of which resulted in fractures. No narratives were provided.)

STRANDED, INADEQUATE EQUIPMENT, WEATHER, EXPOSURE, EXCEEDING ABILITIES
Colorado, Longs Peak

On January 14 at 0900, Mark Swinnerton (34) and Danny Pyatt (34) passed by rangers Kurt Oliver and Jim Detterline at the Chasm Meadows Cabin below the East Face of Longs Peak. The rangers informed the climbers that a storm was beginning, ice/snow conditions were marginal on the peak, and that overnight gear was highly recommended for winter attempts. Swinnerton and Pyatt continued on to attempt Kiener's Route. Slowed by the marginal ice/snow conditions and caught in the storm, they traversed over to the top of the Notch Couloir and spent a brutal night without bivouac gear. Unfamiliar with the descent, they ended up in Glacier Gorge where they were found.

Analysis

Swinnerton and Pyatt sustained minor cold injuries but the results could have been much worse. They did not have adequate clothing or shelter for the conditions. A map and compass and the knowledge of how to put them to good use should also be part of the climber's equipment selection. A search costing several thousand dollars was necessary to solve this particular incident. It included sending out ground searchers and a helicopter into the storm. (Source: Rocky Mountain National Park Rangers)

FALL ON ICE, INADEQUATE EQUIPMENT
Colorado, Boulder Canyon

On February 9, Gary Wheeler (33) fell 15 meters and slid another 30 meters, landing at the base of a waterfall and against a tree.

Wheeler had climbed the waterfall, tied a rope around a tree, and walked down a dirt path to give his partner the one pair of crampons they had. The partner fell several times trying to climb the waterfall, so Wheeler went up the dirt path to adjust the rope. He slipped when he went to adjust the rope. (Source: *The Denver Post*, February 10, 1990)

(Editor's Note: According to Dixon Hutchinson, leader of the Rocky Mountain Rescue Group, this was the first ice climbing death in the area in ten years. One or two die rock climbing in boulder Canyon every year, but not all of these are climbers.)

FALL ON ROCK, PROTECTION PULLED OUT
Colorado, Longs Peak

On April 15, Randy Joseph (33) fell suddenly and without warning during a lead on Longs Peak of Alexander's Chimney. Conditions were mixed thin ice and bare rock, with protection mostly rock devices. Joseph had removed his crampons for a short stretch. He fell about ten meters, pulling out a stopper. Joseph sustained a fractured fibula and displaced tibia on his left leg. His belayer, Jim Scott, assisted him in rappelling three pitches to Lamb's Slide and in struggling to Chasm Lake. While Scott went for help, Joseph crawled to the Chasm Meadows Cabin. Rangers met Joseph at the cabin, and he was flown out from Chasm Meadows on the following morning. (Source: Rocky Mountain National Park Rangers)

Analysis

Joseph is a highly skilled climber and former Longs Peak ranger. His efforts in getting from the climb to the cabin with a painful injury in winter conditions are quite noteworthy. Mixed climbs on large alpine peaks in winter conditions are inherently dangerous. This is an example of a team which was prepared for, and effectively dealt with, an emergency which could have ended up in a fatality for a less qualified team. (Source: Rocky Mountain National Park Rangers)

FALL ON ICE, ICE TOOLS PULLED THROUGH MELTING ICE, INADEQUATE PROTECTION, WEATHER
Colorado, Rocky Mountain National Park, Hallett Chimney

On May 13, my partner and I (32) set out for Hallett Chimney. The weather was warming, and a sunny day expected, following a great many spring snowstorms. This day, temperatures were expected to rise as high as 10 degrees C, although we expected Hallett's north facing chimney to remain colder. The snow was firm for the approach, although it began to turn to corn as we finished the approach to the base at 0730. On the hike in, it was apparent that water on the few exposed rocks on the trail had not completely frozen overnight. Based on our recent visits to the park, and the depth of the snowpack, we expected the snow and ice route to be in prime shape. We were wrong.

The first four roped pitches, which brought us to a belay at the base of the pitch through the chockstone-capped section of the chimney, were challenging and enjoyable. We found secure but sparse protection on the rock. Ice screws were essentially worthless. The ice varied from a softening thin layer on the rock to a thin layer encrusting deep snow. We were occasionally showered by snow melting off the chimney walls. The climbing was well within our abilities, so we were undaunted by the soft ice. It was a beautiful day and we felt good about the climb.

The chockstone pitch was my partner's lead. Notwithstanding his alpine experience, the loose snow and deteriorating ice challenged him. He progressed slowly upward, and established a good belay on the ledge of the steep snow slope just above the chockstone.

Mine was the next lead, the last before easier ground leading to the top. I moved up the snow gully to its top, a snow wall below an ice sheet. The ice sheet encrusted snow which clogged the chimney above. The rock on the chimney walls beneath the snow and ice overhang revealed no possibility of protection. Rather than digging snow away from the chimney's walls, I opted to step up right onto steeper ground with an eye to skirting the insecure ice along a steep rock ramp at the right edge of the ice. Unfortunately, once up a couple of committing and difficult moves to an ice ledge plastered to the rock, my hopes for cracks for protection and more secure climbing were dashed.

Run out for 12 meters from my belay, I now found myself with three depressing options—none of which included protection, all of which held the distinct possibility of a long fall. Down-climbing probably would have been the better choice, though it did not appear so at the time. The rock ramp offered at least three meters of 1.2 cm melting verglass on steep moss-covered, crackless rock. I opted to pull onto the six to eight meter ice sheet, which at least appeared likely to remain affixed to the wall.

I sank my axes into the porous ice, overhead and slightly left, testing them to the extent possible without committing myself. I then committed my weight to their grip. As I lifted a foot toward the bottom of the sheet, just above knee height, both axes pulled through the deteriorating ice. I fell backward, landing approximately ten meters below in the steep snow gully. I attempted to self-arrest, but carried too much momentum. I skidded down the snow toward the chockstone, striking it, then falling through the opening it formed at the top of the chimney. Three or four meters below, the rope stopped my fall. I had taken a frightful 25 meter fall, but, incredibly, could move all of my limbs and collect my thoughts. My right shoulder and ribs hurt, but I was not immobilized.

Chris lowered me to our last belay, and we then began six single-rope-length rappels, and belayed descents of two snowfields. My fall occurred 180 to 200 meters above the base. Once there, I was able to hike out. (Source: John Seebohm)

Analysis
As with all mixed alpine climbs, this climb required judgment calls about changing conditions. There was sufficient snow and ice to climb, but the warm temperature was against us. In retrospect, we may have wrongly ignored early signs of significant warming: water on rocks encountered along the approach which had not frozen overnight, and softening snow, both at the base and on the route. Yet, the weather in the preceding days had been cold, and our climb was north facing. We incorrectly thought it would be in fine shape.

As we progressed up the climb, the lack of secure protection on ice did not greatly concern us. We were able to find sufficient protection along the rock for comfortable climbing, given our abilities. Apparent protection ran out at the point where the melting conditions made for treacherous climbing. It is doubtful that such a fall could have been altogether avoided without turning back. Having chosen to go forward, I might have searched longer for protection prior to committing myself to steep ground which posed as much danger to ascend as to descend.

On the other hand, our experience and safety-consciousness ultimately served us well, although the preceding account might lead one to seriously question whether we had learned anything in our 30 years of combined climbing experience.

A sound belay, established by my partner, held a forceful fall. My helmet likely prevented more serious injury, as I struck the chockstone encountered in my fall with my head, shoulder and ribs. Even with the helmet, it is pure luck that I did not receive greater injuries than a bruised shoulder and ribs.

After the fall, we maintained our composure and effected a safe self-rescue without further mishap. (Source: John Seebohm)

LOSS OF CONTROL—VOLUNTARY GLISSADE, INADEQUATE INSTRUCTION AND SUPERVISION, POOR POSITION
Colorado, Rocky Mountain National Park, Andrews Glacier
On June 14 at 1300, Mike Hill was leading a group of 25 to 30 juveniles from River Valley High School, Spring Green, Wisconsin, in a glissading class on Andrews Glacier. A 17 year old female failed to maintain control, and broke her right fibula while glissading. Hill, a former EMT, initiated a self-rescue with an improvised litter. (Source: Rocky Mountain National Park Rangers)

Analysis
During an interview with Hill, Park Service investigators found out that the group had not been properly briefed before attempting actual glissade practice. The group was also insufficiently supervised, as there were too many students per instructor. The runouts at the base of Andrews Glacier are somewhat dangerous, ending in a deep, cold alpine lake on one part and in talus on another part. This kind of exercise requires (1) doing more prebriefing, (2) having more instructors per student, and (3) using a different, safer location. (Source: Rocky Mountain National Park Rangers)

FALL ON ROCK, INADEQUATE PROTECTION
Colorado, Rocky Mountain National Park, Notchtop

On July 6 at 1600, Ulrich Moderl (22) of Austria took a 15 meter fall from the 5.9 crux pitch of the South Ridge on Notchtop. Moderl sustained a fractured right ankle and pain in his right knee and back. Martin Pircher, Moderl's partner, effected an evacuation and carried Moderl piggyback to the trailhead. (Source: Rocky Mountain National Park Rangers)

Analysis

Running out long alpine pitches with little or no protection increases the chance of injury in the event of a fall. Fortunately Moderl's partner was able to perform an efficient rescue. What can never be understated in the decision for a party to perform a self-rescue is the need for a thorough medical survey. Had the pain in Moderl's back been due to a fractured vertebrae, the three mile piggyback ride could have turned him into a paraplegic. (Source: Rocky Mountain National Park Rangers)

FALL ON ROCK, POOR POSITION, EXCEEDING ABILITIES
Colorado, Rocky Mountain National Park

On August 23 at noon, Marcus Hall (30) took a five meter leader fall from La Chaim, a 5.7 route on the Pear. Hall slipped while he was attempting to clip the first bolt on the route. Jill Wilson, Hall's climbing partner, went to get assistance from Rocky Mountain National Park rangers in effecting a evacuation. (Source: Rocky Mountain National Park Rangers)

Analysis

The act of placing protection is generally the most vulnerable situation a lead climber is exposed to. It is very important for the leader to maintain a wide, stable stance and to keep three points of contact with the rock if possible. On bolt-protected leads, the climber is often tempted to stretch upwards and out of balance in an attempt to clip in before the stable stance that the bolt was drilled from is obtained. Leaders should concentrate on getting a good stance first, and then clipping in second.

This type of accident is more common on rappel-placed routes where the first ascender is not really in contact with good stances. (Source: Rocky Mountain National Park Rangers)

FALL ON ROCK, CLIMBING UNROPED, EXCEEDING ABILITIES, FAILED TO FOLLOW DIRECTIONS
Colorado, Rocky Mountain National Park, Longs Peak

On August 26 at noon, Spencer Hannah (32) and another teacher were leading a group of six juveniles and another teacher from Campion Academy, Loveland, Colorado, up the North Face of Longs Peak. Ranger Jim Detterline warned them not to come up, as they were not equipped and the route was full of ice. Hannah talked the others into climbing, however. But it was Hannah who slipped on icy vegetation and fell 60 meters to the base of the route. He sustained numerous abrasions, contusions, and lacerations, and an open fracture/dislocation of the right ankle. Bleeding was difficult to control and he was given 2000 ml of IV fluid. Climber Mike Daniher rescued the stranded six students. (Source: Rocky Mountain National Park Rangers)

Analysis
Hannah said that he was a 5.4 leader on rock. The North Face route, a 5.4, was at the top of his limit when it was not icy. Conditions were so icy that two other parties on that day elected to do a different crack to the side. With Hannah's knowledge of roped climbing techniques, it is impossible to understand why he would talk seven beginners (some of whom were seriously frightened) into soloing a technical route. The resulting situation involved an all-night technical litter lowering/scree evac/wheeled litter evac for ten kilometers (helicopters were able to land rescuers on the summit but were not able to pick up Hannah), and the roped rescue of the six stranded kids by Danier. (The other teacher had continued to the summit.) (Source: Rocky Mountain National Park Rangers)

STRANDED, DARKNESS, FAILED TO FOLLOW DIRECTIONS
Colorado, Rocky Mountain National Park, Longs Peak
On August 26 at 2200, members of Rocky Mountain National Park's Search and Rescue Team were involved in an evacuation at Longs Peak's Boulderfield when they heard cries for help coming from the False Keyhole area. Volunteers Jim Disney and Brad McCullogh were sent to investigate. They found out that Nancy Richards and Sue W. were stranded in the dark on the False Keyhole, a cliffy ridge-like feature on the North side of Longs Peak. Disney and McCullogh directed the stranded climbers back to the west and out of hazard. (Source: Rocky Mountain National Park Rangers)

Analysis
Richards and her partner had just completed an ascent of the Diamond, the very technical big wall on Longs Peak. However, they did not know their descent route on the Keyhole, and became stranded despite their headlamps and technical equipment. Big wall rock climbers are not necessarily good route-finding alpinists. A little research concerning the descent route(s) might have averted this hazardous situation. Placing a guidebook, map, and compass in one's rucksack can also help to prevent situations like this.

There were several other competent climbing parties who were unable to negotiate their descent routes due to a lack of knowledge in 1990 at Rocky Mountain National Park. Fortunately for the Richards party, the rescue team was in the area, and a potential tragedy or at least hardship was averted. (Source: Rocky Mountain National Park Rangers)

FALL ON ROCK, WEATHER, PROTECTION PULLED OUT, NO HARD HAT
Colorado, Rocky Mountain National Park, Sundance Buttress
On September 6, Richard Jakush (42) and Bill Oswald were climbing Bonzo, a 5.10 route on Sundance Buttress. Jakush was leading the steep, sustained climb, and he took a one meter fall part way up. He continued climbing and near the top it began to rain. Oswald suggested that they back off, but Jakush wanted to complete the route. Jakush placed a piece of protection which fell out as he climbed by. He slipped and fell six meters impacting on the back of his head. Oswald lowered the unconscious Jakush and contacted park service rescue team to perform a long scree evacuation. Jakush sustained a fractured skull and posterior brain contusion. (Source: Rocky Mountain National Park Rangers)

Analysis
Jakush would not back off despite his earlier performance (a fall and a poorly placed protection piece) and the deteriorating weather. Also, he was not wearing a climbing helmet. The serious head injuries he suffered might have been fatal had it not been for Estes Park Ambulance Paramedics Gerry Hickson and Jeff Schanhals who had hiked to the scene and administered medications to control the swelling in the brain. (Source: Rocky Mountain National Park Rangers)

STRANDED, WEATHER, ROUTE FINDING PROBLEM
Colorado, Rocky Mountain National Park, Longs Peak
On September 15, Jim Mauch (33) and Cathy Casey (34) set out to climb Kiener's Route on Longs Peak. Climbing conditions were somewhat icy and the party was slowed down. They spent the evening of September 16 without their bivouac equipment at the base of a 5.6 dihedral about 150 vertical meters below the summit of Longs Peak. A winter-type storm ensued over the next two days and they were unable to climb out. Rangers Jim Phillips and Ken Unitt climbed Kiener's Route on September 18 during a massive search effort. They assisted Mauch and Casey to the summit, where they were flown away in an Army Chinook helicopter with the climbing search teams. (Source: Rocky Mountain National Park Rangers)

Analysis
Mauch was an experienced mountaineer who led rock to 5.8. Longs Peak would be his 54th and final Colorado fourteen thousander to achieve. Casey was relatively a beginner. They became stranded due to the poor weather and poor route finding. There is a 4th class exit to the right of the 5.6 dihedral which is the standard finish for Kiener's Route. To the credit of their survival skills, they certainly did survive two nights out in nasty weather with minimal equipment. It should be mentioned that winter-type storms commonly begin in September at Rocky Mountain National Park, and aspirant climbers should be equipped and experienced to deal with such.

Because this was Mauch's 54th fourteen thousander, there was some over-zealousness involved. The climbers had even packed a bottle of champagne for the summit celebration. (Source: Rocky Mountain National Park Rangers)

STRANDED, DARKNESS, INADEQUATE EQUIPMENT, FAILURE TO LEARN DESCENT ROUTE
Colorado, Rocky Mountain National Park, Taylor Peak
On December 12, Markin Fevughack (25) and Holley English (25) became stranded atop Thatchtop Mountain due to darkness after an ascent of Taylor Glacier on Taylor Peak. It took them most of the following day to work their way down Thatchtop and back to the trailhead. Rescue efforts, including the use of helicopter and numerous ground teams, were then terminated. (Source: Rocky Mountain National Park Rangers)

Analysis
Fevughack and English, although accomplished rockclimbers, had less than a year of snow/ice climbing each. This caused them to have an extremely slow ascent of Taylor

Glacier, topping out at 1600. Possibly a more significant factor here was that they did not research the descent routes and did not have a map and compass. They had concentrated on finding out all they could about the approach (even the shortcuts) and the route with its alternatives. After they topped out, they thought they could descend Thatchtop but got cliffed out and benighted. (Source: Rocky Mountain National Park Rangers)

(Editor's Note: According to David Essex, Chief Park Ranger, the STRANDED and OVERDUE missions in Rocky Mountain National Park were high this year. Three such situations, two of which resulted in fatality, involved scramblers on fairly serious peaks.

Also of note in Colorado were the four avalanche fatalities involving skiers, one of whom was snow boarding. A fifth avalanche accident involved a narrow escape when a solo back country skier, Dakars Gowans (44), was carried a hundred meters down a 37 degree slope into some trees. He was able to crawl back to Lindley Flat, where his friends effected a rescue.

During the past 39 years, according to the Denver Post, 107 people have died in Colorado avalanches. Most of these are probably ski related.)

FALL ON ROCK, NO HARD HAT
Idaho, City of Rocks
On June 25, Tim Herron (early 30s) fell about five meters from Dire Straights. He was held by his rope, but he struck his head. He was lowered to a rock formation below, unconscious and having convulsions. He was evacuated and flown to Pocatello. He died on August 4. (Source: Idaho State Parks and Recreation Accident/Incident Form)

(Editor's Note: This park has become a very popular climbing area. Very few accidents are reported. The ratio of serious injury/fatality to climber days is indicative of the level of expertise which assembles here.)

FALL ON SNOW, CLIMBING ALONE, LOSS OF SKI POLE BASKETS— THEN SKI POLES, STARVATION
Idaho, Mount Borah
In early September, Paul Kovatch (40) began his attempt of Mount Borah. This was his seventh try, and nearly ended his goal of reaching the highest point in each state. Here is a portion of the report he sent:

Dear Sirs of the Accident Booklet:
Were I to give the accident a heading, it would be something like Climbing Alone, Equipment Failure, Loss of Ski Poles, Starvation. The equipment failure was the loss the day before my fall of the round "basket" around the lower part of one of the ski poles. Without that "basket" I couldn't lean on both poles on that 45 degree snowfield. That made the accident almost inevitable. I was coming out of a fairly long, even steeper gully/ chimney, and at first the less steep snow was a relief. Precisely at the base of the snowfield was where the mountain became permanently less steep. For reasons I can't

pinpoint, I didn't stop to figure out the obvious way down—going along the side of the snow, i.e., where it met the rocks. Haste made waste, and away I went. Shock then prevented my being rational enough to effect a successful rescue of the ski poles. Not having the ski poles added at least a week to the ordeal. The first three days after the loss, I had energy. With my ski poles, I'd have been able to walk, slowly and carefully, downhill, into the woods, and out onto a gravel road that I already knew came up to the mouth of the canyon. Few if any hallucinations would have happened, and I probably wouldn't have had to drink urine.

About my rescue, this should be said: I was about to move farther along when those three fellows came marching over the hilltop above me. After going over the route to safety and my car with them, I was going to make it, even had no one been there. I might have been crawling like a worm when I reached the car, but next day I would have reached it.

I couldn't possibly express the look of horror and sympathy on my rescuers' faces when I told them what I'd had to eat and drink.

I will need at least eight tries to reach the summit of Mount Borah. The late Tenzing only needed seven for Everest. Borah is certainly not Everest, but of course, Tenzing was not an amputee. (Source: Paul Kovatch)

LIGHTNING
Maine, Mount Katahdin, Baxter State Park
On August 27, 1990, David Passalacqua (13) was struck and killed by lightning while hiking the Knife Edge near Pamola Peak. He was with a Boy Scout troop consisting of ten Scouts and two leaders. Another Scout and a leader were injured, and all felt the strike, which occurred at 1600 in a brief, but severe, storm. Their location was such that there was no chance for cover for at least another 20 or 30 minutes. (Source: Baxter State Park— Search and Rescue Report)

Analysis
Park officials reported that the Scout troop was experienced, having backpacked many mountains since 1987. The weather report called for a 30 percent chance of showers in the afternoon. The Scouts did not go into the Knife Edge in bad weather. The storm came up suddenly, after they had hiked the Knife Edge Trail and were within 100 meters of Pamola Peak, which is where the strike occurred.

The park Director, Irwin "Buzz" Caverly, indicated that the last recorded lightning strike fatality was in 1968, at Chimney Pond—well below the summits and the timberline. Twenty-two people were marked or affected by that one strike. (Source: Baxter State Park—Search and Rescue Report)

(Editor's Note: While not a climbing accident, this report is included to remind high peaks hikers and climbers in New England of the potential for this hazard. While very few have been killed by lightning in Baxter State Park, the White Mountains, Green Mountains, or Adirondacks, those which have occurred are similar. For instance, in less than 12 months in 1984, an Outward Bound group was struck on Franconia Ridge—causing an instructor fatality—and a man was killed while sitting at a picnic table at the base of Mount Lafayette in Franconia Notch. Both events were during isolated, brief afternoon storms.)

FALL ON ICE, POOR POSITION, INADEQUATE EQUIPMENT, INEXPERIENCE
New Hampshire, Meadows Cliffs—Rumney

On January 27, 1990, Mark Jacobson (23) and Zvi Cohen (22) were ice climbing in the Meadows area in Rumney, New Hampshire. They completed one climb, rappelled off, and began to look for another route. As the temperature had risen above freezing and the cliffs faced the sun, few climbs were in shape. They proceeded to the far right area of the cliff where Cohen soloed a short climb and Jacobson followed with a belay. They then decided to walk along the top of the cliff in the woods to look for another climb or to rappel off. As they were walking in the woods, Cohen decided to take a closer look at two other climbers who were finishing up on Centerfold. Cohen walked closer to the edge of the cliff onto a slab covered with wet leaves and dirt.

The two climbers, Robert Augart (23) and John Morris (21), saw Cohen and warned him that it was not safe to stand there. Cohen responded by turning around and taking a few steps back up the ledge, when he slipped and fell onto his side. He was unable to arrest his slide, since he was not wearing crampons or carrying an ice ax. He fell approximately 25 meters, and was knocked unconscious. Morris rappelled down to see if Cohen was all right. He did not respond, so Morris ran to his car and drove to a nearby house and called for help. Jacobson walked down the side of the cliff as Cohen was carrying their only rope. Jacobson met the rescue team and led them to the victim. During the rescue a large part of Centerfold collapsed, nearly hitting Cohen and the rescue team. Despite the fact that Cohen was less than 200 meters from the road when he fell, it took over an hour to get him to the road. He died several hours later in a hospital in Plymouth. (Source: Robert Augart and Mark Jacobson)

Analysis

Cohen had been rock climbing for two years, but this was his first season of ice climbing. He had picked up the technique of vertical ice climbing very quickly and was confident in leading. He had less experience in evaluating changing conditions and terrain. More winter climbing experience might have led Cohen to reconsider his position at the edge of the cliff, or at least to wear his crampons or carry an ax in hand. (Source: Robert Augart and Mark Jacobson)

AVALANCHE
New Hampshire, Mount Washington, Tuckerman Ravine

On March 30, 1990, the Mount Washington area received about 20 cm of new snow, with winds greater than 65 kph from the south. The winds continued through the night.

At 0800 the next morning, with 20-40 cm of overnight wind deposited snow noted in gullies and catchment areas, USFS Snow Rangers stationed in Tuckerman Ravine posted avalanche hazards as "HIGH", unchanged from the previous day, for all the skiing routes above the Little Headwall." This information is prominently displayed in two places: at the trailhead by the AMC base camp in Pinkham Notch, and at the Hermit Lake shelter at the base of the ravine.

At 1000, a nearby gully (Express) avalanched spontaneously. About the same time, we observed a solitary skier, carrying his skis, climbing near the top of Left Gully, which rises about 275 meters from the floor of the ravine toward the southwest. Two additional skiers were about 180 meters below him. Because of the highly unstable conditions, and the cornice at the top of the gully, we monitored the progress of the three closely. The average slope was about 30 degrees and was steeper at the top where it ran into the cornice.

Our radio reported that another gully (Dodge's) avalanched naturally, just as the uppermost skier was putting on his skis below the cornice. He then started descending traverse and initiated a turn on the 40+ degree slope. Immediately, the entire upper third of the gully erupted in a soft slab avalanche, leaving a 35 cm crown line.

The dust cloud obscured vision from below while the slide ran the full length of the gully. Scouring the snow cover down to the sliding surface of frozen granular, the slide split into two deposition zones, each about 75 meters long, 40 meters across, and five meters deep at the toe. We observed the entire episode to take about nine seconds. The distance traveled was about 600 meters, thus the slide had an average velocity of 240 kph.

The skier was sitting on the snow at the upper end of the left deposition zone. Other than having the wind knocked out of him, there was no evidence of immediate or developing trauma. He was unscathed except for bruises and loss of a ski. We saw that his trajectory took him across a large boulder that split the slide. During the slide, he was tumbled and intermittently buried, and was convinced he would not survive.

As the day progressed, four additional large avalanches were observed, with three of them initiated by skiers. By sheer good luck, none was directly involved. (Source: Roger Damon, Jr., Mount Washington Ski Patrol, NSPS National Avalanche Instructor)

Analysis
The victim's awareness of avalanches was nil, and he had not noticed either of the sign-boards posting the current assessment of avalanche hazard. The two skiers below him were far enough to the right side to avoid involvement. They continued their ascent, and were a cause for concern for some time.

To avoid such accidents, one needs to have: (a) an appreciation of the effects of terrain, weather, and wind that combine to create avalanche hazards, and (b) skills in individual conduct in avalanche-prone terrain, including avalanche recognition, route selection, safety precautions, using islands of protection, carrying location indicating devices, mutual observation, and immediate actions if a party member is avalanched.

This episode involved a solo skier who was above anyone who would have observed his "last seen point." Thus, had he been buried, a successful rescue would have been arduous at best.

It typifies the avalanche accidents that usually result in injury and/or fatality. It also highlights our unique situation in Tuckerman Ravine, where usage is counted in the thousands of people on a busy weekend. Some of those believe that posted warnings are obviously meant for people other than themselves. (Source: Roger Damon, Jr., Mount Washington Ski Patrol, NSPS National Avalanche Instructor)

(Editor's Note: This is not a climbing accident, but is presented as an example of how skiers used to groomed ski areas can quickly get in trouble when out of that controlled mountain environment.)

FALL ON ROCK, NO HARD HAT
New Hampshire, Cathedral Ledges
On May 9, two climbers were going up Standard on Cathedral when the leader fell from Cave Wall about 1700. He suffered a concussion and felt lower back pain. The

New Hampshire Mountain Rescue Service did the carryout. (Source: George Hurley, Mountain Guides Alliance)

Analysis
There have been several accidents at the Cave Wall, one other this summer. The route is graded 5.6 but it's hard for the grade and the crux (the Cave Wall) is impossible to protect well. A .5 Tricam will fit in an old piton hole but it is marginal as protection. The other option is to avoid the wall by climbing as deep in the chimney as possible, placing pro in the chock stones. (Source: George Hurley, Mountain Guides Alliance)

FALLING ROCK
New Hampshire, Cannon Cliff
In May, a climber was injured by rockfall on the upper part of Union Jack on Cannon. Other climbers have reported loose rock on Cannon, including on the Whitney-Gilman arete, Fugue, and Vertigo. Routes on Cannon are more dangerous than most routes of the same grade on cliffs at lower elevation. Of the seven deaths on Cannon, five have involved loose rock. (Source: George Hurley, Mountain Guides Alliance)

PROTECTION PULLED OUT, FALL ON ROCK
New Hampshire, Cathedral Ledges
On July 31 a leader was having trouble getting into the lower of the two V slots on Double Vee (9+) on the upper left wall of Cathedral. He placed a small TCU (three cam unit) and hung from it. As he pulled up on the TCU, it pulled out. In the nine meters of crack below there were two nuts. The highest also pulled out. The other nut was a #1 wire which took some of his weight as the climber hit the ledge and probably kept his injuries from being worse. He broke his left wrist and compressed his thoracic vertebrae. (Source: George Hurley, Mountain Guides Alliance)

Analysis
Protection at the top of this route is difficult to place and the climbing is awkward. More and better protection just below the V slots would have helped. (Source: George Hurley, Mountain Guides Alliance)

(Editor's Note: A New Hampshire winter hike turned into a mountaineering event. While on a winter traverse of the Presidential Range in December, a woman suffered a broken leg when she fell against a rock. The accident happened just below Thunder Storm Junction, 1.9 km from Gray Knob, in a rain storm with winds around 110 km per hour. She and the rest of the party, under the able guidance of Bill Aughton, were wearing crampons for the snow, ice, and frozen ground. It took 13 hours to complete the rescue.)

FALL ON ROCK, EQUIPMENT FAILURE
New Mexico
Recently, an REI customer had an accident while rock climbing in which a carabiner broke. (He was not injured, fortunately.) The customer returned the carabiner to the Albuquerque store, and our testing lab examined the carabiner to find out what went

wrong. This story explains some of the problems that were discovered—you may want to share the prevention information with your customers in the future.

The customer slipped when he came to the top of a rock pitch. When the force of his fall came on the protection a meter below, he felt only a quick jerk as a carabiner broke, and he plummeted until his next piece of protection held. Instead of a short fall, he took a heart-stopping nine meter fall. He was shaken, but fortunately not seriously injured.

Why did the carabiner break? Similar ones (the carabiner was not an REI one) had tested just fine in the REI Test Lab, a result Quality Control Engineer Cal Magnusson confirmed with further analysis after the accident. So what happened? This is what we learned.

The non-locking carabiner returned to our Albuquerque store was in two pieces. By examining the two parts, seeing how they fit together, and comparing with other carabiners tested to the point of destruction, Cal concluded that the carabiner's gate was not closed when the total force of the fall came on it.

Closed carabiners are strong, especially in their long direction, usually 4,000 pounds (1800 kg) or more. But open carabiners are much weaker, sometimes holding only 1,000 pounds (450 kg) or less.

Why did the carabiner open? There are three possibilities.

The first is that the carabiner wasn't properly closed to begin with—the sling or rope was stuck in the gate.

The second possibility is that the carabiner was opened during the fall by the rope or sling twisting over the gate at the moment of impact. This can occur when the protection is at an odd angle, and usually results in the carabiner becoming unclipped.

A third prospect is that the snap of the fall banged the carabiner against the rock, whipping the gate open just as the rope came tight. To see how this can happen, take a carabiner and rap it on your hand. Just when it hits, the gate will come open. If the timing and forces are just so, this can happen when the carabiner takes the fall.

Rock climbers love uncertainty, but not in their carabiners. While we are still uncertain why this one was open, these are some of the lessons to be learned.

- Make sure every carabiner is properly closed. Listen for the characteristic "click" as they are placed. Visually inspect them.
- Make sure that every anchor system is free of funny twists or turns that could cause abnormal loading on the carabiners. Imagine what a fall would do and construct or modify your set up accordingly.
- If you see the possibility of a carabiner banging against the rock, use carabiners with stiff gates. Better still, use two carabiners with gates opposed or a locking carabiner.

Fortunately, carabiner failure is rare; however, it is not unknown. Be careful. And share the information with your customers to be certain they understand what can occur when rock climbing. (Source: Bill Summers article in *Compass*, January 1990. REI monthly employee publication)

FALL ON ROCK, NUT PULLED OUT, NO HARD HAT
New Mexico, Sandia Mountains

On September 16, Jim Ladd (40) and John Wright (39 had underestimated the time for approaching the South West Ridge route on the Needle (they had left the car at 1100) as they were having a difficult time locating the beginning of the route, elected to start up a gully on the formation to get some climbing in, though they didn't expect to be able to top out. On leading the first pitch, Ladd encountered what he estimated as a 5.5 mantle onto a ledge. Just as he completed the move, both hands "popped" off the ledge and he fell 12 meters on sloping ground and was held by his belay and a Lowe Tricam. He hit his hip half way down, fracturing it, and sustained other injuries, including a blow to the head, which made his "head spin" for a few minutes after the fall. His companion climbed to his position and then lowered him to a more substantial ledge. After stabilizing Ladd and leaving spare clothes, Wright went for help about 1600. A friend of Ladd's, Colin Messer, arrived at dusk with food, water, spare clothes and a blanket. Personnel from Albuquerque Mountain Rescue Council, Sandia Search and Rescue and the 1550th Combat Air Crew Rescue School, who had been involved in another rescue that afternoon, began arriving at 1700 with a sleeping bag and medical gear. Rescuers arrived throughout the night with more technical rescue gear. At first light, Ladd was placed in a pair of MAST pants to stabilize his pelvis and loaded into a litter. He was lowered on steep sloping terrain to a site where he was winched into a hovering helicopter from Kirtland Air Force Base and flown to a hospital. (Source: Steven Patchett, Albuquerque Mountain Rescue Council)

Analysis
Ladd stated that he should have protected the move better. Protection closer than three meters away could have prevented the injuries. He also felt that they should have carried more gear for a forced bivy, though that did not contribute to his injuries. Finally, he was very lucky to have suffered only a "spinning" sensation after his head contacted the rock during the fall. A hard hat would have minimized his chances of a serious or fatal head injury.

Ladd was given a prescription pain killer by Messer when he arrived on the scene. Utmost caution should be administered in administering such a drug to a subject with possible head injuries. The dangers of pain killers in such cases outweigh their usefulness and should only be used by medical personnel trained in their use. (Source: Steven Patchett, Albuquerque Mountain Rescue Council)

FALL ON ROCK, FAILED TO FOLLOW ROUTE, EXCEEDING ABILITIES, PLACED INADEQUATE PROTECTION, PROTECTION PULLED OUT
New Mexico, Sandia Mountains, Muralla Grande
Dave Kilgore (36), Don McIntyre (44), and Steven Patchett (39) were climbing the La Selva route (5.7) on Muralla Grande in the Sandia Mountains near Albuquerque, New Mexico. Patchett had taken the second lead and gotten off route at the end of the pitch. Kilgore took the third lead and elected to traverse across to the route, rather than downclimbing the easier ground below, to regain the line. The ascending traverse became increasingly difficult, but he continued, thinking the difficulties would ease up, and that some of the moves would be hard to reverse. When he fell, around 1300, a group of three steel nuts, about two meters behind him, all pulled (he knew they were questionable) but a piece six meters below held and he stopped after falling 12 meters, hitting a couple of ledges on the way. Kilgore was lowered to a ledge a meter below, and was then joined by McIntyre and Patchett who downclimbed to his position. Kilgore suffered severe contusions to his buttocks, elbow and wrist, and was quite shocky and incapacitated by his injuries. The two climbing ropes were tied together and Patchett lowered Kilgore, with McIntyre alongside, 90 meters down the vertical,

sometimes overhanging terrain below. Patchett rappelled the route to rejoin the two, after which McIntyre went for help. More than 40 members of Albuquerque Mountain Rescue Council, Sandia Search and Rescue and the 1550th Combat Air Crew Rescue School responded, pulling Kilgore up the steep terrain of Chimney Canyon to Sandia Crest, where Kilgore was loaded into an ambulance at 1630 the day after the accident. (Source: Steven Patchett, Albuquerque Mountain Rescue Council)

Analysis
Kilgore was off route on much more difficult terrain than the normal route. He was climbing at the top of his ability and with questionable protection behind him. We all do it. Most of the time, we get away with it, and come away pumped with another great story. He didn't get away with it this time.

All the individuals involved are active members of Albuquerque Mountain Rescue Council and experienced mountaineers. They had the equipment and knowledge to quickly evacuate the injured man to the base of the climb. Pick your climbing partners well!

One might consider one of the benefits of membership in a Search and Rescue organization. No one turns down a call when it's "one of our own"—probably for the chance to "rib" the subject during the evacuation! (Source: Steven Patchett, Albuquerque Mountain Rescue Council)

VARIOUS FALLS ON ROCK, MOSTLY NO OR INADEQUATE PROTECTION
New York, Shawangunks
In 1990, there were 20 climbing accidents, one of which was fatal, 12 of which resulted in fractures. The fatality resulted when a 15 year old boy slipped while at the top of the Cliffs and fell over 40 meters. He and his father were there for "recreational rappelling." Again, lead climbers with inadequate protection constituted the majority of the injuries—12.

Among the unusual occurrences were (a) a 56 kg person attempting to lower a 91 kg male—resulting in a 15 meter fast ride and burned belayer hands; (b) a man dislocating his shoulder from trying to reach out and stop a friend who was falling; (c) a woman being hit on the lip by falling protection that a leader on an adjacent climb had dislodged; and (d) a man falling 12 meters because he thought he was being belayed when he was being lowered off a 5.13. He was not. (Source: Mohonk Preserve)

(Editor's Note: The case where the climber thought he was being lowered may happen more frequently, both on natural climbs, which are extremely difficult and being attempted several times by the same climber, and on artificial walls. Belaying in these circumstances is usually done totally without using the standard climbing calls—in fact, it is usually done with no calls. The assumptions made are not always correct.)

FALL ON ROCK, INADEQUATE BELAY, NO HARD HAT
North Carolina, Moore's Wall
On June 9, 1990, as a party of four, we were planning to lead and follow the route, Golden Earring, a 5.7. The first two members of the party had already led up a short 15 meter pitch. Joe was then belayed up from the top. Since the difficulty was very

minor, Joe belayed Cameron up the same climb. The rope was properly anchored at the top. In a standing position, Joe proceeded to belay Cameron with a figure eight connected to his harness. He was not separately anchored. Cameron climbed with an extra rope. He slipped on a wet spot about two meters up from the start of the climb. Cameron's fall pulled Joe off balance. Joe fell face first over the rock. Cameron fell to the base of the climb. Cameron's weight held Joe from sliding down the slope. (He was still attached to the rope by the figure eight.)

Cameron fell and swung into a small tree, with no injury. Joe skinned his left arm and left leg and hit his head just above the left ear, immediately resulting in double vision. Joe never lost consciousness and was soon able to right himself and secure himself. With the aid of the rope Cameron was able to safely climb to Joe and lower him to the base of the climb. (Source: Joseph Hanna)

Analysis
First of all, we both decided that the accident was caused by a lack of common sense, but more because of the lack of difficulty involved. Seeing no present danger, we overlooked the obvious in eagerness to continue the latter half of the climb.

Nevertheless, the system was not checked with understanding. A helmet would have eliminated the seriousness of the injury but would not have prevented the accident. The belayer should have been secured separately, regardless of whether or not he felt secure.

The Climbers Guide to North Carolina and previous knowledge of the area allowed us to reach medical care within a reasonable amount of time. We will continue to be aware of medical services in the area in which we climb and in the future, helmets are a must! (Source: Joseph Hanna)

WEATHER, HYPOTHERMIA, AMS
Oregon, Mount Hood
On June 9, Cassandra Kelley (38) was transported from the 3000 meter level on the south side of Mount Hood to Timberline Lodge. She was with a Mazama group, and was experiencing altitude sickness and hypothermia symptoms on the ascent. The group continued to the summit, where they experienced high winds and blizzard conditions. Clackamus County searchers were called at 1330 and found the group at 1608 using a locator unit which fixed on the beeper being carried by the group. (Source: from a story in the Sunday Oregonian, June 10, 1990)

(Editor's Note: No information on how or why a rescue team was called in was included in the report. Beepers are being used by many groups on Mount Hood now, as a result of the 1986 blizzard in which nine persons from the Oregon Episcopal School died.)

FALLS, FALLING ROCK, NO HARD HAT
Pennsylvania, Delaware Water Gap N.R.A.
There continues to be more climbing and off-trail hiking in this reservation. Two of the three reports we received involved rappels. In May, a 17 year old female was climbing up a hill with several other members of her group to do some rappelling

when a large rock was knocked loose from above and struck her on the right side of her head. In September, an 11 year old Boy Scout was engaged in a rappelling experience with his father and several others when he "appeared to slip, then screamed and disappeared from sight," of the adults at the top. Rangers climbed up to him—just seven meters from the bottom of the rappel—and found that he had just made a sideways swing, which had scared him. No injury resulted, and it was observed that the activity was being run safely. (We did not count this as an accident.)

The other fall involved a couple who were making their way back to the road by way of a bank beside a creek. The woman, Elizabeth Taylor (30), fell 40 meters, hitting a rock and losing consciousness. This, while not a climbing accident, resulted in a technical climbing rescue. (Source: Reports, submitted by Jim Yestor, came from the Delaware Water Gap N.R.A.)

FALLS ON ROCK, PROTECTION PULLED OUT, NO HARD HAT, ETC.
Utah, Cottonwood Canyons
Four reports of climbing accidents were filed for this area, one resulting in a fatality when a solo climber fell while descending Mount Superior's north side. The others resulted in injury due to the length of the falls. (Source: H. Thad Moore, Salt Lake County Sheriff's Office)

WEATHER, EXPOSURE, EXCEEDING ABILITIES
Washington, Mount Rainier
During the week of March 19-23, 1989, a ten-person Special Forces Unit of the U.S. Army climbed from Paradise to the Camp Muir area and back for the purposes of testing equipment and men in a winter mountaineering and survival environment. Three members were sent back to Paradise at 1200 on March 21 because two of them, SSGT Bronn (28) and SFC Taylor (36), were suffering from various degrees of hypothermia, frostbite, and fatigue. SFC Martinez, a medic, was assigned to look after them. The party encountered blizzard conditions and a near white-out. Progress was very slow, with two men on skis and the third on snowshoes. For reasons unexplained, some of the equipment that would have assisted with navigation down the snowfield was given to a member of the seven-person unit continuing to Camp Muir. The three became disoriented and descended Paradise Glacier instead of Muir Snowfield.

The group of three encountered continued severe weather the next day. Despite the danger of travel on glaciated terrain, they chose not to rope together. In fact, they traveled closely bunched together in order not to get separated from each other.
At 2200 they stopped for an extended period to melt snow for water, soup, etc. They did not set up a tent or dig a snow cave to spend the rest of the night, choosing instead to continue walking slowly. They were not able to return to Paradise on either the 21st, as expected, or the 22nd.

The evening of March 22 and the morning of the 23rd plans were made and teams organized to search for the overdue party. Just as three park rangers and 15 volunteer Seattle and Tacoma Mountain Rescue people were about to initiate a ground search, the three soldiers arrived back at Paradise at 0500. Bronn was later treated for second degree frostbite to his lower back and toes and Taylor for a back injury. The remainder of the Special Forces Unit successfully descended from Camp Muir to Paradise in clear weather without further incident, although two individuals were reported suffering from some degree of frostbite. (Source: George Sainsbury)

Analysis
We concluded that the personnel on the training mission had flunked navigation, passed survival, and flunked communication. (Source: George Sainsbury, Paul Williams, Seattle Mountain Rescue Council)

FALL ON ROCK, INADEQUATE EQUIPMENT, FATIGUE
Washington, Icicle Creek Canyon
This accident occurred on April 15 while I was participating in an Intermediate Rock 1 climbing course field trip with the Mountaineers. The subject of the class was the placement of protection and leading.

The morning and early afternoon was spent placing protection while top-roped on the three main cracks of Flake Slab. In the afternoon, while leading for the first time, I fell from near the top of the Middle Crack while attempting to move up. At the time of my fall, I was probably not more than two meters beyond my last piece of protection. However, the Middle Crack ascends diagonally, and I fell onto the rounded top of an adjacent flake below the Middle Crack. My protection held and the belay absorbed part of the force of the fall; my rib cage absorbed the rest. (Source: Jim Green—46)

Analysis
Climb with good climbing shoes, and place protection effectively. Had I not been wearing a climbing helmet, I may have suffered a head injury as well. (Source: Jim Green)

FALL ON ROCK, CHOCK PULLED OUT, INADEQUATE PROTECTION, INEXPERIENCE
Washington, Icicle Creek Canyon
On April 15, I could not complete a lead in mid-afternoon and was down climbing/being lowered when the top protection pulled out. The chock hit me in the right eyebrow, breaking my glasses, causing a nose bleed and unconsciousness. I fell four to five meters to hard ground landing on my left side and then rolled onto my face. I was unconscious for about a minute, and thought I was reasonably coherent. I have no recall of events for 20 minutes. Other injuries were a bruised left elbow and fractures of three to four transverse processes from the left side of the lumbar vertebrae. Others in the group called EMS in Leavenworth and the Mountaineers trip leader. I was splinted for back injury and quickly transported to the hospital. (Source: Frank Rossi— 47)

Analysis
If one cannot complete leading a pitch, place additional protection, and downclimb as much as possible. Do not rely on being lowered. Wearing a hard hat and eye glasses undoubtedly prevented further injury. I was unconscious from being hit by the chock, causing me to be relaxed when I hit the ground. Four weeks later I was backpacking again. (Source: Frank Rossi)

FALL ON ROCK, PROTECTION PULLED OUT, INADEQUATE PROTECTION
Washington, Icicle Creek Canyon

The accident occurred on April 29, during the final hours of a two day rock climbing training session for intermediate students from the Everett Branch of The Mountaineers. The weather was warm and sunny. Rock conditions were excellent. The students were practicing climbing leads in the vicinity of Mountaineers Crack, a popular training area in the Icicle Canyon near Leavenworth.

The victim, Karl (45), and his rope partner, Roy (27), were attempting to climb a section of low to mid fifth class crack. One of the instructors, Larry, was giving general supervision of the climb from a nearby fixed rope position. Both climbers had led climbs of similar difficulty during the course of the weekend and at other times and were comfortable and confident with the conditions encountered.

A belay station was established at the base of the climb. The first four meters of climb consisted of a moderately inclined fourth class face which the climbers had no difficulty in negotiating. No protection was placed in this area which later proved to be a contributing factor to the severity of the injuries sustained. The next four meters involved a crack climb in which the crux move was the initial meter where the flaring, wide crack made jamming difficult and few face holds were available for hands or feet. Roy attempted to lead the route and placed the first piece of protection, a large hex placed end ways, about head high in the crack, six meters above the belay station. The hex appeared bomb proof for a downward pull. After about ten minutes spent attempting to negotiate the crux move, the two climbers exchanged places. Having checked the protection, Karl began climbing and also experienced difficulty with the crux move. After a number of false starts, he succeeded in moving a meter or so up the crack so that the hex was near waist height. While attempting to move past the protection, Karl's fist jam above the piece failed and in falling backwards and out of the crack he dislodged the lone piece of protection.

Without any protection for the rope, Karl cartwheeled down about 25 meters, striking the ledge at the start of the crack, and from there bounced down the inclined lower face and landed among the boulders at the base of the climb near Roy. Help came immediately from the six other students and two instructors, all of whom were experienced in mountaineering first aid. Karl, who was unconscious for several minutes following the fall, suffered a concussion, broken bones in his cheek and thumb, a severe shoulder sprain and minor leg abrasions. His climbing helmet undoubtedly saved his life judging from the severe damage it sustained. After regaining consciousness, he was able to walk to the nearby road from where he was transported by ambulance to the hospital in Leavenworth. He was discharged several hours later following various repairs. Two subsequent surgeries and several months of recuperation were required before he could resume climbing. (Source: The Mountaineers)

Analysis

As with most climbers, both Karl and Roy had fallen numerous times while testing the limits of their climbing skills. Until the accident, the protection they had placed had always been sufficient to stop the falls and prevent any serious injuries. Here they did not see the risks posed by not backing up the one piece of protection for a difficult move. Neither climber foresaw the consequences of an outward or upward pull on the hex. Since the serious portion of the climb began only a meter below the hex, the easy lower face was disregarded as a potential hazard and no protection was placed in this part of the pitch.

Two other factors may have contributed to the accident. First, it was late in the second day of climbing and both were somewhat fatigued and therefore less attentive. Secondly, the climbing up to this point had been both challenging and successful, which probably led to both climbers being in a somewhat overconfident state of mind. The same factors may have led to the instructor's failure to notice their error in not placing enough protection. Both climbers have since returned to climbing, somewhat wiser.

One very significant lesson learned by those involved in this incident was the importance of wearing a proper helmet when rock climbing. Without it this accident would most likely have resulted in the climber's death or permanent disablement. (Source: The Mountaineers)

FALL ON ROCK, FALLING ROCK, NO HARD HAT, EXCEEDING ABILITIES
Washington, Index—Town Wall
On May 5, after freeclimbing two-thirds of the way up the route, we encountered water dripping down the face. We continued to climb up into the chimney. Mike freeclimbed up and then sent down a rope. He had me on belay as I climbed the chimney, back to one wet wall, feet to the other wet wall. About three to four meters up, I slipped. On belay, I hung there, but when the rope went tight over the edge, it released the rocks that struck me. The first rock hit my head, then my shoulders, then the rope on the rocks below. The second rock hit my head and along with the rest of the rocks, hit, cut and ruined the rope below. My head stung—then it felt wet—then it started to drip. By ten seconds after the rocks first fell, Mike called to find out what happened. I told him I was bleeding and to let me down. He couldn't see me and he couldn't hear me very well. Below us other climbers were coming up. One pretty close, one farther down, and one at the bottom. Between them they could hear both of us. Not being able to see me or know the severity, one went to town and sounded an alarm. The climber closest to me called out that he was in a position to climb up if necessary. It took Mike about one and a half to two minutes to let me down. I thought the best idea was to get to the closest climber below before blood loss became a factor. The cut was bleeding at a fair flow and I could not stem it. I rappelled about 15 meters to the climber who was already well anchored in. We were on a good ledge to rest. A helicopter appeared, spotted us, hovered for a moment, and landed. The climber put me on belay, and I rappelled down to another climber. I stayed on the first rope and finished the descent. Waiting at the bottom was the rescue team. (Source: Chuck Amon—27)

Analysis
Basic knowledge and attention to safety in rock climbing would have prevented this accident. Use ropes, use a helmet, and don't climb wet rock. (Source: Chuck Amon)

LOSS OF CONTROL—VOLUNTARY GLISSADE, INADEQUATE EQUIPMENT AND INSTRUCTION, EXCEEDING ABILITIES
Washington, Stevens Pass Ski Area
While practicing head-first glissade and self-arrest procedures with a group of 40 students and 14 staff from an Everett Mountaineers Scramblers course on May 16, 1990, Brian Fletcher (16) lost his grip on his ax and could not regain control. In the slide either the spike or pick end of the ax sliced a small cut across his chest and made a puncture wound near his stomach, just missing vital organs in the abdomen. He was rescued using the ski area's grooming machine for transport. (Source: Neil Johnson)

Analysis
Snow conditions were very hard at the time of the accident. Fletcher had practiced this arrest many times the previous day, but in soft snow. With hard snow conditions, the slope might have been too aggressive for students with one day of experience. Also, there needs to be more emphasis on buying gloves and axes that allow students a good grip on the spike end of the ax.

There seems to be considerable confusion about the best way to do the head-first-on-the-stomach arrest. Different instructors and different books say different things. We think more research needs to be done to establish good principles for this arrest. (Source: Neil Johnson)

(Editor's Note: This accident, and the July 28 accident on Mount Baker, reflect the range but by no means the full number of glissade incidents reported this year in Washington State. From the hard snow to soft snow conditions shown here, from fortunate minor injury to unfortunate fatality, the accounts of problems glissading were too numerous to include other than in the actuarial data.

Various analyses accompanying the reports raise an equally wide range of issues, from suggestions to avoid axes with ring loops to the dangers of using no ax at all to reminders to avoid the lure of the easy way down.)

FALL ON SNOW, WEATHER, EXCEEDING ABILITIES, INADEQUATE EQUIPMENT
Washington, Snoqualmie, Silver Peak
On June 17, this accident occurred while a party of 11 "Alpine Scramblers" were descending Silver Peak. Lori Levin (30) reported the following:

The leader and the group were in a hurry to get home due to fog and rain. The snow was especially icy and slippery. I tried to keep up and overstepped a hill and fell (45 meters) into a tree off a cliff. My ice ax slipped out of my hand so I could not self-arrest. I screamed and fell. A half hour later I was rescued and walked out OK after rescue help. (Source: Lori Levine)

Analysis
I will always secure my ice ax with a wrist loop and I will never go on a trip when I am exhausted from a stressful week. The conditions of bad weather, being inexperienced and afraid helped make the trip difficult. I won't go on advanced trips when I am a beginner. I won't climb if I've had a bad week, and I will only do easy scrambles. (Source: Lori Levin)

HAND-HOLD AND ROCK ANCHOR CAME OUT, FALL/SLIP, OFF ROUTE
Washington, Mount Thompson
On July 22, five climbers left base camp between Mount Thompson and Bumblebee Pass at 0500 for a Mountaineer's led climb of the West Ridge. Steve Sulzbacher led the party, with Diane Magyary assistant leader and designated first aid leader. Other members included Randy Johnson, Bruce Gaulke, and Kathy O'Toole (27). All climbers were wearing hard hats and seat harnesses, though no one was using a chest harness.

The third pitch appeared to go up a gully, which Gaulke led with some difficulty. They concluded that the "correct" route was actually to the left of this gully. O'Toole saw a way up there, and Sulzbacher set up to belay her. O'Toole placed four chocks as she climbed the pitch. Her fifth point of protection was a runner around a sizable rock horn. She was two to three meters above this runner when a handhold pulled out and she fell, pulling a boulder one meter in diameter with her. The rock horn also failed and pulled out. Chocked protection below arrested her fall. She landed upside down, still secure in her seat harness, but suffered a fractured ankle. O'Toole was able to assist in rappelling down to base camp though later had to be evacuated by MAST helicopter. (Source: Compiled from reports by Steve Sulzbacher and Kathy O'Toole)

Analysis
I was climbing a crack system with a fair amount of moss. I perceived the significance of the moss but chose to continue climbing. As the system was more difficult than the route was supposed to be, I concluded I was off route. I fell when I weighted a handhold and the rock broke off.

I landed head down, back against the mountain, but didn't fall out of my harness because I'd been taught to tighten the waist belt as much as possible, which kept me secure even upside down. My belayer and climbing leader commented that it was fortunate I'd opposed my first two chocks, so as to prevent zippering. The entire party was very supportive. I'm very grateful to the training the Mountaineers provided all of us. It came in handy. (Source: Kathy O'Toole)

LOSS OF CONTROL—VOLUNTARY GLISSADE, FALL INTO CREVASSE, IMPROPER CLOTHING, NO HARD HAT
Washington, Mount Baker
On July 28, 1990, a party of 11 was on three ropes descending the Roman Wall on Mount Baker. At the crest, the team led by Earl Crouse (63) waited for the other two teams to arrive from the pyramid at the summit. When all had arrived, the lead team started down the very steep part of the Roman Wall. Weather was excellent, but the snow was very soft. They followed a deep trench made before by several rope teams, assuming the two teams above would follow behind them in the same trench.

About halfway down, a call came that the second rope team, following a different route and led by Tom Knudsen (39) had fallen into a crevasse. Due to rapid warming, snow surface had softened and broke loose, making arrest of descent difficult. One person on the rope team, William Knudsen (42), had stopped short, but the other three slid into a crevasse two to three meters deep.

The leader, Tom Knudsen, was buried deep in a trench at the back of the crevasse in snow carried in with him in the fall. The second person on the rope team, a 12 year old boy, was buried in a foot of snow, but hollered; the third man in had landed standing up and was able to quickly uncover the boy's face so he could breathe. The fourth man, the boy's father, did not get dragged into the crevasse.

It later took an hour and a half to dig Tom Knudsen out. He was found to have expired, probably from a blow to the head in the fall. Snohomish Country SAR helicopter later assisted Bellingham Mountain Rescue personnel in recovering Knudsen's body. (Source: Earl Crouse and William Knudsen)

Analysis
The first three on the team involved were wearing slick outer pants like ski warm-ups, which made glissading very fast, easily out of control. The fourth man, who managed

not to fall in, was wearing wool pants. The snow was very soft, making it difficult if not impossible to self-arrest with ice axes. However, there were four other paths where parties had glissaded in exactly the same spot. Their path was in the center of these four, so probably it seemed safe to try coming down the "easy" way.

In retrospect, I should have been very specific about the danger of glissading, especially at the top of Roman Wall, and explained that you must: (1) be under total control; (2) be 100% certain there are no crevasses below; (3) take note of the kind of clothing you are wearing when glissading. Also, protective head gear would likely have prevented serious injury. (Source: Earl Crouse and William Knudsen)

SLIP ON SNOW, CLIMBING UNROPED, FAILURE TO FOLLOW INSTRUCTION
Washington, Mount Adams
On August 4, 1990, at 0500, a party of three was climbing a moderate slope in stable snow above a crevasse about 3000 meters on Mount Adams' Mazama Glacier. The weather was fair, light winds, low 30 degree temperature. Lee Kelly (58), the leader, and Bonnie Bronson (50) were experienced climbers, though the level of the third member, Mark Stevenson (41) was not known. It was the judgment of Kelly to climb unroped as the slope was approximately 30 degrees and snow conditions were excellent. For reasons unknown, Stevenson suddenly sat down in the snow and started sliding. Bronson stepped out and attempted to stop his fall but was knocked down and slid with Stevenson into the crevasse. In the uncontrolled fall, he landed on top of her. Bronson died instantly of a broken neck. Stevenson sustained a dislocated shoulder. Evacuation was accomplished at 1700 by the combined efforts of three different area mountain rescue units and two Chinook helicopters from Fort Lewis. (Source: Compiled from reports by Lee Kelly, Central Washington Mountain Rescue, and Yakima County Sheriff's Office)

Analysis
Stevenson sat down unexpectedly, contrary to instructions, and as he began to slide he made no attempt at self-arrest. Though experienced, Bronson tried to stop him without self-arrest. I should have been more alert to the mental condition of Stevenson. (Source: Lee Kelly)

(Editor's Note: We don't know whether these climbers knew each other. In any case, the victim either didn't understand or follow instructions. Also, any assumption—rather than knowledge—of levels of competence can lead to complications.)

FALL ON ROCK, PROTECTION PULLED, NO HARD HAT
Washington, Snoqualmie Pass, The Tooth
On August 11, Creth Edward Cupp (31) and Joanne Metzler were climbing the last pitch of the Southwest Face of the Tooth, 5.6, when leader Cupp fell 25 meters pulling two pieces of protection before being arrested. Metzler lowered Cupp, who had severe head injuries, three pitches to a large ledge at the top of the first pitch where Cupp could no longer continue. After spending the night on the ledge, Metzler descended to the Denny Creek trailhead notifying King County Police at 0830 on August 12. Seattle Mountain Rescue was paged by KCP at 0850.

The subject was reached by team one at 1300. A MAST Chinook and Huey helicopters were on scene, and with SMR's Base Operations Leader Mike Maude as spotter, located the rescue party. The craft was low on fuel, but was able to hoist the subject along with SMR's Critical Care Nurse, Diane Eldrenkamp. Both helicopters returned to Alpental, transferred the patient and Eldrenkamp to the Huey which transported the patient to Harborview Trauma Center. (Source: *Trage*, Fall—1990)

SLIP ON ICE, NO HARD HAT
Washington, Mount Baker
While descending Mount baker around 2000 meters via Coleman-Deming Glacier on September 9, Steven Amber (27), Vincent Willard (25) and Reese White (29) approached the last slope directly above their tent site on the Hogback at 1700 after a successful climb. White was leading a roped descent, Amber in the middle, and Willard last. As they entered a crevassed area, Steven Amber slipped and fell. Willard turned into the ice and went into self-arrest position. As he swung his pick into the slope, the ice fractured away, and he too was pulled off his feet. His wrist loop was not around his wrist, and he immediately lost his ice ax. The two rolled a few meters and fell into a crevasse. Willard was knocked unconscious; Amber's fall was arrested before hitting bottom, and he was able to climb out unassisted.

Reese White immediately rappelled down and began treating Willard's head wound. Three other climbers in the camp below had witnessed the fall and climbed up to aid the injured party. Two of them stayed the night with White and Willard while the third member escorted Amber back to the camp. Authorities were notified of the accident. Willard and Amber were evacuated by helicopter the following morning at 0730 and treated at St. Joseph's Hospital in Bellingham. Willard suffered a fractured skull and ankle and compression fracture of the spine, Amber a fractured wrist and broken nose. (Source: Compiled from reports by Steve Amber, Vincent Willard, and Whatcom County Sheriff's Office)

Analysis
In late season ice conditions, it would be advisable to take an easier route. We could have gone around the ice entirely. It would have taken an hour longer, but the accident wouldn't have happened. We talked to two other climbers the day before, and they had gone around the ice on their descent. We also had two ice screws along, but to save time didn't use them. A helmet would have spared me my head injury. Sharper crampons and ice ax might have helped, too. P.S. Does this mean we get a free copy of 1990 Accidents in North American Mountaineering? (Source: Steven Amber and Vincent Willard)

(Editor's Note: Falling into a crevasse is not the recommended method of attempting to secure a copy of ANAM. Membership in the American Alpine Club is the best way to avoid the retail price.)

AVALANCHE, WEATHER
Washington, Dragontail Peak
Eric Simmonson (22) and his partner (22) left the parking lot at Colchuck Lake early on the morning of November 3 to climb Dragontail's north face in a day. The pair climbed up high on the route but decided to quit and descend the route because of freezing rain

and snowfall. The weather had deteriorated. The pair was unroped and down climbing when an avalanche hit them. Eric was thrown off his stance and fell approximately 300 meters down the couloir. His companion escaped being struck by the avalanche and was safely able to down climb the route. He thought Eric was killed by the avalanche. Eric also thought his partner was dead and managed to crawl down approximately 60 meters below the entrance of the gully before his companion reached him. The two climbers did not have any bivouac gear. A partial snow shelter was built for the victim and his partner left to go seek help. On his way down he encountered two hikers who were on their way up to Asgard Pass. He recounted the story of the accident. The climber proceeded out to notify the sheriff's department. The hikers reached the victim at 1430. They found the victim uncontrollably shivering. All his clothes were wet. They set up their tent, stripped him of his clothes and placed him in one of their sleeping bags. The victim told them he spit up some blood after the accident and was complaining of internal pains.

At 2300 two members from Central Mountain Rescue arrived. One was a paramedic. The victim was placed on an IV and given medication. Everyone spent the night just below the couloir. The medic noticed that the victim passed blood in his urine in the morning.

At 0700 on November 4, a team of 20 people was assembled at the PUD district station in Leavenworth by the sheriff's department to provide a carry out. At 1030 the carry out team reached the victim and at 1115 the carry out began with the victim placed in a litter. High winds, snowfall and lack of visibility persisted. At 1400 the victim had been moved to the lower end of the Colchuck Lake. A decision was made to continue transporting the victim down the trail. An Air Force helicopter from Spokane was put on alert with the idea of positioning it at the fish hatchery area on Icicle Creek Canyon. The weather continued to deteriorate. At 1600 the Stuart Lake-Colchuck Lake trail fork was reached. The helicopter was now positioned in Icicle Creek. Weather still made it insufficient for a fly-by. Fifteen minutes were requested to hold further transport in order to assess a "scrub or go" on a helicopter pickup at the swampy meadows just above the trail fork. The weather cleared slightly and the pilot/sheriff's department decided to do a fly-by and check conditions.

The helicopter landed and litter carriers were forced to ford a very cold Stuart Creek above waist level. The victim and medic were placed aboard the helicopter and transported to Wenatchee State Hospital. The victim's injuries were determined to be fractured vertebrae, broken ribs, and a broken thumb. (Source: Seattle Mountain Rescue Council)

Analysis
Eric and Cal felt the snow conditions in the lower and middle couloirs were stable at the time of the avalanche. They believe the avalanche started either in the upper (third) couloir or resulted from snow breaking loose from a ledge on the face that rises above the left side of the Hidden Couloir. They believe that being roped would have been no advantage in this situation.

The route description in Becky's guide warns of avalanche danger. (Source: Fred Stanley)

RAPPEL ANCHOR INADEQUATE, NO BELAY, NO HARD HAT
West Virginia, Cooper's Rock State Forest
On Saturday, July 21, 1990, Dan Audley (31), Marty Donahue and six Boy Scouts stopped on their way home from Camp Mountaineer to do some rappelling. They

were joined by Scott Gray and Adam Dugas. The cliff where they planned to do the rappelling is 18 meters at its highest point. It offers a good vertical surface on which to rappel.

Two rappel ropes were placed, both secured to trees. Donahue went down the rope first followed by three of the Boy Scouts. Audley then attempted to descent on the same rope. Donahue is quoted as saying, "And somehow the carabiner snapped and the rope came down." Audley fell the full 18 meters.

Dugas climbed back to the highway where he flagged down Deputy Sheriff Mark Ralston and a process server Darris Summers. Dugas and Summers remained at the highway to await Emergency Medical Service units to arrive. Ralston proceeded to the scene where he performed CPR on Audley for about 25 minutes. According to the newspaper four ambulances and over 25 rescue personnel responded to the accident as well as some members of the Cheat Lake Volunteer Fire Department. The EMS crews were practicing vertical rescue techniques at the time at a quarry when the call came. Upon arrival they "performed full advanced life support procedures." The CPR and other measures were to no avail. He died of massive head injuries. (Source: Compiled from the July 22, 1990, Sunday edition of the *Dominion Post* newspaper (Morgantown, WV) and a telephone interview with Chief Bran Dean, Rescue Chief of the Monongalia County EMS, who was present on the scene of the accident and investigated the death. Submitted by Dr. James Patrick Mace)

Analysis
According to Bran Dean, Rescue Chief of the Monongalia County EMS, Audley was the leader of the party and professed knowledge of climbing. It was he who rigged the two rappels, one 15 meters and the other 18 meters. Only one rappel setup was intact when the rescue team arrived. This was not the rappel that failed. The fatal rappel was taken apart by persons on the scene before the rescue team arrived. However, the intact rigging indicated the procedures used by the victim when he rigged the ropes. According to Dean, this rappel was rigged with a single doubled sling wrapped around a tree with the end loops secured with a single non-locking carabiner. The sling was tied together with a single square knot without the ends being tied and was not tied around the tree. The rope was attached to this rigging with a figure eight on a bight knot clipped to the sling with another single non-locking carabiner. There was no secondary anchor or sling placed as a backup to this rappel rigging.

Chief Dean and his colleagues believe the accident was caused by a bad anchor setup. The fatal rappel came completely away from the tree on which it was rigged. According to the report of the other rappellers, the victim wrapped a doubled sling several times around a tree at the top of the rappel. He tied a figure eight on a bight into the middle of the rappel rope and clipped into the sling on the tree using a "locking" carabiner.

Several people used the rappel prior to the victim. They were young Boy Scouts and another adult who weighed considerably less than the victim, who weighed about 114 kg. The rappel rig came away when the victim tried it for the first time. It was reported that the entire anchor was still attached to the victim when the other adult came to his aid at the bottom of the cliff. Somehow the anchor sling detached from the tree.

Three possible reasons could have resulted in the sling detaching from the tree: (1) The "locking" carabiner was not properly closed and locked or it worked loose while the other rappellers used the system. It opened and released the sling when Audley put his weight on it. (2) No locking carabiner was used (none was used on the rappel left intact). The system failed when a carabiner opened from rope movement. (3) It is possible that in placing the webbing around the tree the victim wrapped it several times but did not connect the end loops together with the carabiner. He may have only clipped the carabiner through the wraps around the tree, thus leaving the sling open to be pulled off the tree. With the sling wrapped several times around the tree, friction held the rope for the others who were lighter than the victim. The sling's friction could not support his weight as it did for the others and it unwrapped when he placed his full weight on it.

It is debatable whether or not a helmet could have saved Audley's life, but people have survived falls of that height before because of this precaution.

Tying the sling around the tree with proper knots, tying a second sling as a backup and tying the rope directly into the two slings would have greatly improved the safety of the system. As the rappel was going to be used over and over, it would have also been wise to tie into another anchor. If non-locking carabiners are used then two carabiners should be used, and their gates opposed in order to prevent the rope from slipping out. (Source: Dr. James Patrick Mace)

(Editor's Note: It is an accepted and common practice to belay all rappels—especially in group exercises of this type. Even leaders and guides are belayed unless there is an emergency, or the guide is the last one down, as would occur in descending a mountain.)

FALLS ON ROCK, ETC.
Wisconsin, Devil's Lake State Park
Three reports of climbing accidents—and several of hikers/ walkers who got into climbing situations—were sent in for 1990. One fatality occurred when a 62 year old college professor fell about 38 meters as a result of a large piece of the rock on which he was climbing breaking free. Another serious injury occurred to an apparent 20 year old neophyte who "lost control" of a rappel he was doing and fell a few meters, landing on a rock. (Source: Devil's Lake State Park—Visitor Accident Reports)

FALL ON ROCK, CLIMBING UNROPED, INEXPERIENCE
Wyoming, Grand Teton
About 2400 on June 26, Stephen Stenger and Arthur Leech (34) left the Lupine Meadows trailhead intending to attempt a one day ascent of the North Ridge of the Grand Teton. They registered their climb with the Jenny Lake Ranger Station.

They encountered difficult conditions on the route. They climbed as high as the "Chockstone," about three or four pitches above the top of the Grandstand. At this point they decided to abandon their attempted ascent and retreated back to the top of the Grandstand. From there, they descended unroped down the Grandstand toward the Teton Glacier. They encountered mixed conditions of soft snow and wet, slippery rock.

About 30 vertical meters from the top of the glacier, Stenger, who was in the lead, thought he heard a strange sound. He turned around and could not see Leech behind him any more. Stenger continued downclimbing, reaching the top of the glacier at the base of the Grandstand. He found Leech, who had fallen over a 30 meter high vertical cliff, landing on the snow of the glacier.

Stenger found his partner semi-conscious, writhing and moaning. Blood was coming from Leech's nose and mouth. He had sustained an obvious serious head injury. Leech was clothed only in polypro tops and bottoms with a nylon shell. His climbing helmet was still on his head. Stenger spent a few brief minutes with Leech, before taking off at a run to summon help. He reached the valley floor and telephoned the sheriff's office at 2228.

The evacuation plan called for using the Lama to shorthaul Leech from his point of rest to a helispot on the lower end of the glacier. He was then to be transferred into the ship and flown to Lupine Meadows. A BK-117 helicopter, with medical flight crew, would then transport him directly to the Eastern Idaho Regional Medical Center.

The Lama arrived at Lupine at 0620. At 0637, a sling load containing the shorthaul pre-rig litter was sling loaded to the accident site. At 0722, Leech was lifted from the accident site and shorthauled to the helispot on the lower portion of the glacier. He was then flown to Lupine Meadows, arriving at 0732. Leech was transferred to the BK-117 which departed for Idaho Falls at 0741.

Leech was admitted to Eastern Idaho Regional Medical Center suffering from facial fractures, a pneumothorax, a concussion and numerous wounds to the skin. Due to the intervention the night before, his rectal temperature was 37.2 C. (Source: Peter Armington, Ranger, Grand Teton National Park)

Analysis
It is extraordinary that Leech survived his fall. The fact that he lay on snow seriously injured with minimal clothing for about seven hours before the first rangers arrived on scene makes his survival even more remarkable.

He wore a climbing helmet, which remained on his head after the fall. The helmet was seriously damaged and no doubt contributed to his survival.

Leech had minimal experience in serious alpine climbing. The Grandstand was covered with snow broken with wet, slippery and loose rock. It is unknown what actually caused him to fall, although he was wearing a heavy pack. His and his partner's decision not to rope the descent almost proved to be fatal. (Source: Peter Armington, Ranger, Grand Teton National Park)

LOSS ON CONTROL—VOLUNTARY GLISSADE, INADEQUATE EQUIPMENT
Wyoming, Tetons, Lower Saddle
On July 27, Shawn Callahan (31) lost control during a voluntary glissade on the snow below the Lower Saddle, near the base of
Middle Teton. An Exum Mountain Guide, Peter Krantz, reported the accident, indicating a possible broken leg.

At 1400 Rangers Carr and Dorward were flown to just above the accident site (southwest of Garnet Canyon Caves) at an elevation of 3200 meters by Kjerstad Helicopters. Ranger Irvine was also flown to the scene from Amphitheater Lake.

The Rangers arrived at the scene shortly thereafter and determined that Mr. Callahan had a 6-8 cm long head laceration and a possible open fracture with obvious deformity of the lower right leg.

At 1620, as the Yellowstone Helicopter was arriving at Lupine Meadows, a second accident occurred at the same location. John Schall, a hiker, had slid 60 meters on snow and slammed into some rocks.

At 1658 additional medical supplies were flown to the scene on the short haul line, during the hover check phase, by the Mountain Rotors helicopter for use in the evacuation of Mr. Schall.

Mr Callahan was short hauled, with Ranger Berkenfield as spotter, from the scene to the Garnet Canyon Meadows at 1710. Mr. Callahan was then transferred to the Kjerstad helicopter and flown directly to St. John's Hospital in Jackson, Wyoming, with Ranger Martin attending, arriving at 1724.

Mr. Callahan was diagnosed at St. John's Hospital as having a compound tibia/fibula fracture, which required surgery, and a scalp laceration. (Source: Jim Woodmencey, Ranger, Grand Teton National Park)

Analysis
In a phone conversation with Mr. Callahan on July 28, I was told that he was descending from the Lower Saddle of the Grand Teton, after a failed solo attempt on the Exum Ridge, at 1030.

Mr. Callahan stated that he was glissading down the snow near the base of the Middle Teton, south and west of the trail near the caves in Garnet Canyon, when his right heel caught on hard snow or a submerged rock. His leg snapped, he lurched backward and hit his head on a rock.

Mr. Callahan also stated that he stopped in place and was able to drag himself to some nearby rocks. He then yelled for help and was soon met by other climbers in the area. Peter Krantz and Peter Lenz, M.D., administered first aid. Krantz descended to report the accident and Lenz remained with the victim until rangers arrived.

Mr. Callahan stated that he did not have an ice ax with him. (Source: Jim Woodmencey, Ranger, Grand Teton National Park)

FALL ON ROCK, CLIMBING UNROPED, PARTY SEPARATED, PROBABLE THOUGHT PROCESS IMPAIRMENT
Wyoming, Tetons, Grand Teton
On September 16 at 1100, Russ Soderlund (40) was climbing the Owen-Spalding route on the Grand Teton with a friend, Gretchen Rupp. Soderlund and Rupp left the Owen-Spalding route above the rappel station and traversed the southeast side of the mountain, near the Exum ridge, to continue to the summit from there. Soderlund continued down a 5.4 friction slab, then continued out on a more difficult face. About the 4100 meter level, he slipped and fell onto a ledge, landing on his heels, with his body leaning backward. He continued to fall approximately 20 meters to another ledge where witnesses saw him sustain fatal injuries. He continued to fall, hit another ledge, and continued into the Ford Couloir where he slid to a point approximately 60 meters above the top of the Petzoldt ridge on the west side of the couloir where he came to rest. He came to rest approximately 60 meters above the toe of the snow, falling approximately 180 meters total to about 3900 meters.

At least three other climbers were in the vicinity of Soderlund when he fell. Austin was next to Soderlund when he fell and Coletti was 30 meters below and to the west. After watching Soderlund fall, Coletti, who was soloing, continued to the summit of the Grand Teton, saw that Rupp was safe with another climber (Scott Cole, a Jackson Hole Mountain Guide), and from there ran down to Jenny Lake Ranger Station where he reported the accident to Ranger Tory Finley. The body was sling loaded from the site at 1912. (Source: Tory Finley, Ranger, Grand Teton National Park)

Analysis
Ms. Rupp stated they had signed out for the Owen-Spalding route and everything was going according to plan until they reached the bottom of the "Owens Chimney." At this juncture, Soderlund stated he wanted to take a different route other than ascending the chimney. This route was about a five minute traverse around the south side of the mountain and across some large slabs of rock. Soderlund stated he had ascended and descended by this alternate route both times he had climbed the Grand Teton. Rupp stated about five to ten minutes after leaving the chimney they came to a location on the southeast side of the mountain which was "very exposed"—slabs of rock were sloping outward and downward and fading into a sheer exposure. At the top of the slabs were a male and a female roped up.

While she was on the summit ridge, she was contacted by a Jackson Hole Mountain Guide. He asked if she was the woman who had just broken up with her climbing partner to take separate routes. When she indicated this was true, he told her Soderlund had probably fallen to his death. Scott offered to permit her to join his group and make the descent and she accepted. She was contacted by Ranger Martin about the time they arrived at Lupine Meadows. The following was learned.

Rupp has had quite a bit of experience in third and fourth class climbing and extensive experience in second class. She has done some technical climbing.

She stated that Soderlund had lived in Aspen for quite some time and had made ascents of many of the 4200 meter peaks in Colorado. She believes he had had about the same level of experience as she. She had never seen him with any type of technical climbing equipment since he had lived in Montana. She had known him for about four years, but Soderlund first came to Montana about seven or eight years ago.

She stated Soderlund was in outstanding health. He was a golf course supervisor and much of his work was physical. He used a pair of old leather Raichle climbing boots for climbing. It was her impression he was a very deliberate person and she felt he was prudent and careful.

Soderlund made the traverse across the slabs without any protection. They had not taken ropes with them, thinking to turn back if the climb got "too dreadful."

Rupp watched Soderlund make the traverse across the slabs and then she hollered down to him that she was not going to attempt it. The traverse was probably 30 feet across and down. Soderlund hollered back that it was "OK"—he would go ahead and make the ascent this way and Rupp could go back and try the chimney route and they would meet on the summit. So Rupp went back and climbed the chimney by herself. The ascent of the chimney took her about half an hour.

An interview with the decedent's sister revealed the following. Ms. Soderlund stated that her brother had been involved in two very serious bicycle accidents in the last six years, both of which involved head injuries which required extensive hospitalization.

The first occurred approximately six years ago in which the doctors told him that he should never ride a bicycle again. The reason was that he had suffered a severe skull fracture and brain injury that led to a form of amnesia. The doctors felt that if he fell or was thrown from a bicycle, it could kill him.

The second accident occurred approximately one and a half years ago when he was struck from the rear by an automobile while riding his bicycle. He was thrown to the ground and suffered a major concussion that required two weeks of hospitalization.

Ms. Soderlund said the accumulated injuries from these two accidents resulted in her brother being moderately disoriented when he involved himself in activities that required even minor thought processes. Ms. Soderlund provided an example: "Russell was driving her down a street that he was unfamiliar with. He would insist he knew where he was going and that he had been on that street before. When it became apparent to him the destination to which he was driving was not there, he became very frustrated and finally realized he was on the wrong street."

Ms. Soderlund went on to say that he was aware of his permanent impairment and therefore was very meticulous about everything he did. Usually his being meticulous compensated for his thought process impairment. Ms. Soderlund felt that is definitely not out of the realm of possibility and in fact very probable that when he began to advance on the fatal climb, he thought he was on a route that he had free climbed previously and would be able to successfully accomplish the feat.

Ms. Soderlund finished our interview by saying she felt he was disoriented on the climb and that disorientation probably led him to attempt climbing a route in which there was no chance of success. She stated that based on her observation of his past disorientation and statements from witnesses in this accident, she was not surprised that he had fallen from a route that he may have thought he was familiar with. (Source: William Miller and Donald Coelho, Rangers, Grand Teton National Park)

(Editor's Note: This tragic fatality is difficult to categorize and even to count as a mountain climbing event. It is included to alert everyone who has—or knows someone who has—a concussion history to heed the advice provided.)

FALL ON ROCK, EXCEEDING ABILITIES
Wyoming, Fremont Canyon

TW (36) and EO (37) planned a weekend (in August) of climbing in Fremont Canyon. They arrived on Saturday morning at 0900. To start the day TW rappelled to the sloping ledge just above the river at the bottom of the canyon below the route Hemateria, then proceeded to set up a belay anchor. After the anchor was set up, EO rappelled down to join TW. Next, TW proceeded to lead Stone King. This route involves a difficult traverse to a small pedestal at the base of an arete. Tom made the traverse and was about four meters up the arete when he took a leader fall. Because of the traverse, rope stretch and the fact that EO was pulled off the belay ledge, the total distance of the fall was six to seven meters. There was no problem with the protection or the belay anchor. In the process of falling, TW's ankle struck the pedestal which resulted in a fracture. At this point both TW and EO were hanging over the river. TW was hanging from his protection with EO holding him on belay. EO was hanging from the anchor. EO was able to climb back onto the ledge while holding TW on belay. EO then proceeded to throw a loop consisting of the slack part of the rope to TW which he used to pull himself onto the belay ledge. TW was unable to climb out of the canyon on his own. They had brought a pair of mechanical ascenders but had conveniently left them in the car. They decided that EO should climb out, get the ascenders, and return rather than use Prussik loops. This was because TW had little or no experience using

Prussik loops. EO climbed out by way of the route Hemateria with TW belaying, and returned with the ascenders. TW climbed out and then EO climbed out without further incident. EO then drove TW to the doctor.

Analysis
TW shouldn't have tried to lead a route as hard as Stone King right off. This is especially true considering the fact that neither EO nor TW had been to this climbing area before. When going to a new area, you should start off on a climb well within your abilities to get a feel for the area's ratings. (Source: TW and EO)

TABLE I
REPORTED MOUNTAINEERING ACCIDENTS

	Number of Accidents Reported		Total Persons Involved		Injured		Killed	
	USA	CAN	USA	CAN	USA	CAN	USA	CAN
1951	15		22		11		3	
1952	31		35		17		13	
1953	24		27		12		12	
1954	31		41		31		8	
1955	34		39		28		6	
1956	46		72		54		13	
1957	45		53		28		18	
1958	32		39		23		11	
1959	42	2	56	2	31	0	19	2
1960	47	4	64	12	37	8	19	4
1961	49	9	61	14	45	10	14	4
1962	71	1	90	1	64	0	19	1
1963	68	11	79	12	47	10	19	2
1964	53	11	65	16	44	10	14	3
1965	72	0	90	0	59	0	21	0
1966	67	7	80	9	52	6	16	3
1967	74	10	110	14	63	7	33	5
1968	70	13	87	19	43	12	27	5
1969	94	11	125	17	66	9	29	2
1970	129	11	174	11	88	5	15	5
1971	110	17	138	29	76	11	31	7
1972	141	29	184	42	98	17	49	13
1973	108	6	131	6	85	4	36	2
1974	96	7	177	50	75	1	26	5
1975	78	7	158	22	66	8	19	2
1976	137	16	303	31	210	9	53	6
1977	121	30	277	49	106	21	32	11
1978	118	17	221	19	85	6	42	10
1979	100	36	137	54	83	17	40	19
1980	191	29	295	85	124	26	33	8
1981	97	43	223	119	80	39	39	6
1982	140	48	305	126	120	43	24	14
1983	187	29	442	76	169	26	37	7
1984	182	26	459	63	174	15	26	6
1985	195	27	403	62	190	22	17	3
1986	203	31	406	80	182	25	37	14
1987	192	25	377	79	140	23	32	9
1988	156	18	288	44	155	18	24	4
1989	141	18	272	36	124	11	17	9
1990	136	25	245	50	125	24	24	4
Totals	3871	564	6847	1223	3306	446	969	195

TABLE II

	1951–1989			1990		
Geographical Districts	Number of Accidents	Deaths	Total Persons Involved	Number of Accidents	Deaths	Total Persons Involved
Canada						
Alberta	241	73	534	20	3	40
British Columbia	224	88	486	5	1	10
Yukon Territory	29	25	63	0	0	0
Ontario	26	6	50	1	0	0
Quebec	18	5	49	3	0	0
East Arctic	7	2	20	0	0	0
West Arctic	1	1	2	0	0	0
Practice Cliffs[1]	13	2	18	0	0	0
United States						
Alaska	267	93	824	8	3	18
Arizona, Nevada Texas	44	5	75	0	0	0
Atlantic –North	491	79	750	24	2	43
Atlantic–South	34	8	54	4	2	10
California	730	204	1588	32	4	49
Central	71	5	119	3	1	4
Colorado/Oklahoma Montana, Idaho	483	156	797	19	4	41
South Dakota	45	20	67	3	2	4
Oregon	94	51	234	1	0	4
Utah, New Mexico	78	31	140	8	1	11
Washington	725	231	1266	27	4	48
Wyoming	373	79	653	7	1	13
Practice Cliffs[1]	362	98	143	3	0	5
Artificial Walls	1	0	1	0	0	0

[1]This category includes bouldering, as well as artificial climbing walls, buildings, and so forth. These are also added to the count of each state and province, but not to the total count, though that error has been made in previous years. Tables I & II still do not correlate because of this. Correct figures are being worked on.

(Editor's Note: Artificial Walls may become a part of the report from now on.)

TABLE III

	1951–89 USA	1959–89 CAN.	1990 USA	1990 CAN.
Terrain				
Rock	2727	330	93	13
Snow	1744	262	38	8
Ice	130	56	6	4
River	12	3	0	0
Unknown	19	6	2	0
Ascent or Descent				
Ascent	2433	341	80	13
Descent	1552	232	53	11
Unknown	237	45	3	1
Immediate Cause				
Fall or slip on rock	1764	163	73	12
Slip on snow or ice	615	123	23	6
Falling rock or object	387	99	11	2
Exceeding abilities	305	27	7	0
Avalanche	227	93	3	0
Exposure	193	12	3	0
Illness[1]	191	14	3	3
Stranded	169	38	7	0
Failure of Rappel	141	21	1	0
Loss of control/voluntary glissade	139	12	7	1
Fall into crevasse/moat	104	33	2	1
Failure to follow route	88	18	4	0
Piton pulled out	69	12	0	0
Faulty use of crampons	49	4	1	0
Nut/chock pulled out	43	3	5	0
Lightning	36	5	0	0
Skiing	34	9	1	0
Ascending too fast	32	0	0	0
Equipment failure	4	2	1	0
Other[2]	79	11	10	0
Unknown	48	8	0	0
Contributory Causes				
Climbing unroped	772	103	16	15
Exceeding abilities	733	126	17	8
Inadequate equipment	451	54	10	1
Weather	289	31	5	2
Placed no/inadequate protection	280	29	33	5
Climbing alone	260	42	6	5
No hard hat	131	18	24	0
Nut/chock pulled out	121	8	12	2
Darkness	96	12	3	0
Piton pulled out	78	10	1	0
Party separated	77	15	5	0

	1951-89 USA	1959-89 CAN.	1990 USA	1990 CAN.
Contributory Causes (cont.)				
Poor position	51	8	11	0
Failure to test holds	49	13	2	0
Exposure	48	9	2	0
Inadequate belay	39	5	7	0
Failed to follow directions	42	1	3	2
Illness[1]	26	4	1	0
Equipment failure	6	2	0	1
Other[2]	138	30	14	11
Age of Individuals				
Under 15	97	11	2	0
15-20	1037	176	12	5
21-25	1190	204	32	2
26-30	767	152	28	9
31-35	413	76	28	0
36-50	531	83	36	2
Over 50	77	11	7	1
Unknown	697	300	25	31
Experience Level				
None/Little	1309	233	24	7
Moderate (1 to 3 years)	1160	248	27	12
Experienced	991	274	36	5
Unknown	1029	195	54	1
Month of Year				
January	140	7	3	0
February	149	30	4	1
March	203	33	5	1
April	256	23	11	1
May	526	36	16	1
June	647	38	26	1
July	756	182	25	7
August	660	184	19	9
September	944	35	16	2
October	259	27	3	0
November	127	3	6	0
December	49	14	2	2
Type of Injury/Illness (Data since 1984)				
Fracture	391	43	67	15
Laceration	178	14	37	5
Abrasion	106	8	10	4
Bruise	94	11	11	5
Sprain/strain	95	10	11	0
Concussion	45	6	10	0
Frostbite	38	0	7	3
Hypothermia	36	5	2	5

	1951-89 USA	1959-89 CAN.	1990 USA	1990 CAN.
Dislocation	26	3	8	0
Puncture	15	2	0	0
HAPE	31	0	3	0
Acute Mountain Sickness	9	0	1	0
CE	4	0	1	0
Other[1]	90	19	12	0
None	22	3	0	0

[1]These include: a) infection; b) posterior brain contusion; c) ruptured spleen; d) pneumothorax; e) teeth knocked out/broken; f) amnesia.

[2]These include: a) miscommunication several); b) inadequate instruction and supervision; c) ice ax strap problems; d) distraction; e) inappropriate technique.

MOUNTAIN RESCUE GROUPS IN NORTH AMERICA
(Area covered in parentheses)
°Indicates membership in Mountain Rescue Association

ALASKA
Alaska Mountain Rescue Group,° P. O. Box 241102, Anchorage, AK 99524 (Alaska
U. S. Army Northern Warfare Training Center,° Fort Greeley, AK, APO Seattle 98733

ALBERTA
Banff Park Warden Service, Banff National Park, P. O. Box 900, Banff, Alberta
    T0L 0C0 (Banff National Park)
Jasper Park Warden Service, Jasper National Park, P. O. Box 10, Jasper, Alberta
    T0E 1E0 (Jasper National Park)
Kananaskis Park Warden Service, Kananaskis Provincial Park, General Delivery,
    Seebe, Alberta T0L 1X0 (Alberta outside National Parks)
Waterton Park Warden Service, Waterton National Park, Waterton, Alberta T0K 2M0
    (Waterton National Park)

ARIZONA
Arizona Mountaineering Club Rescue Team, P. O. Box 1695, Phoenix, AZ 85030
    (Arizona)
Central Arizona Mountain Rescue Association,° P. O. Box 4004, Phoenix, AZ 85030
    (Central Arizona)
Grand Canyon National Park Rescue Team,° P. O. Box 129, Grand Canyon, AZ 86023
    (Grand Canyon National Park)
Southern Arizona Rescue Association, Inc.,° P. O. Box 12892, Tucson, AZ 85732
    (Southern Arizona)

BRITISH COLUMBIA
Columbia Mountain Rescue Group, Royal Canadian Mounted Police, Invermere,
    B.C. V0A 1K0 (East Kootenays)
Glacier Revelstoke Park Warden Service, Glacier Revelstoke National Park, P. O. Box
    350, Revelstoke, B.C. V0E 2S0 (Glacier Revelstoke National Park)
Kootenay Park Warden Service, Kootenay National Park, P. O. Box 220, Radium Hot
    Springs, B.C. V0A 1M0 (Kootenay National Park)
Mountain Rescue Group, c/o Frank Baumann, P. O. Box 1846, Squamish, B.C.
    V0N 3G0 (Coast Range, Northern Cascades)
North Shore Rescue Team,° 165 East 13th Street, North Vancouver, B.C. V7L 2L3

CALIFORNIA
Altadena Mountain Rescue Team, Inc.,° 780 E. Altadena Drive, Altadena, CA 91001
    (Los Angeles County)
Bay Area Mountain Rescue Unit, Inc.,° P. O. Box 6384, Stanford, CA 94309 (Northern
    Sierra Nevada)
China Lake Mountain Rescue Group,° P. O. Box 2037, Ridgecrest, CA 93555
    (Southern Sierra Nevada)

De Anza Rescue Unit, P. O. Box 1599, El Centro, CA 92243 (Imperial Valley, Baja, California)

Inyo County Sheriff's Posse,° P. O. Box 982, Bishop, CA 93514 (Inyo County)

Joshua Tree National Monument SAR,° 74485 National Monument Dr., Twenty-nine Palms, CA 92277

June Lake Mountain Rescue Team,° P. O. Box 436, June Lake, CA 93529

Los Padres Search and Rescue Team,° PO Box 30400, Santa Barbara, CA 93130

Malibu Mountain Rescue Team,° PO Box 222, Malibu, CA 90265

Montrose Search and Rescue Team,° PO Box 404, Montrose, CA 91021 (Los Angeles County)

Riverside Mountain Rescue Unit,° PO Box 5444, Riverside, CA 92517 (Riverside County)

Saddleback Search & Rescue Team, PO Box 5222, Orange, CA 92667

San Diego Mountain Rescue Team,° PO Box 81602, San Diego, CA 92138

San Dimas Mountain Rescue Team,° PO Box 35, San Dimas, CA 91733

San Gorgonio Search & Rescue Team, San Bernardino Sheriff, San Bernardino, CA 92400 (San Bernardino Mountains)

Santa Clarita Valley Search and Rescue,° 23740 Magic Mountain Parkway, Valencia, CA 91355

Sequoia-Kings Canyon National Park Rescue Team,° Three Rivers, CA 93271 (Sequoia-Kings Canyon National åPark)

Sierra Madre Search and Rescue Team,° PO Box 24, Sierra Madre, CA 91025 (Southwestern United States, Baja, California)

Yosemite National Park Rescue Team, Inc.° PO Box 577, Yosemite National Park, CA 95389 (Yosemite National Park)

COLORADO

Alpine Rescue Team, Inc.° PO Box 934, Evergreen, CO 80439 (Front Range)

Colorado Ground Search and Rescue,° 2391 S. Ash Street, Denver, CO 80222

El Paso County Search & Rescue, Inc.,° PO Box 9922, Manitou Springs, CO 80932 (El Paso County)

Eldorado Canyon State Park,° PO Box B, Eldorado Springs, CO 80025

Garfield Search & Rescue,° PO Box 1116, Glenwood Springs, CO 81602

Grand County Search & Rescue,° PO Box 172, Winter Park, CO 80482 (Grand County)

Larimer County Search & Rescue,° PO Box 1271, Fort Collins, CO 80522 (Larimer County)

Mountain Rescue—Aspen, Inc.° PO Box 4446, Aspen, CO 81612 (Western Slope)

Ouray Mountain Rescue Team, PO Box 220, Ouray, CO 81427 (Gunnison National Park, Rio Grande National Forest, Uncompahgre Park)

Rocky Mountain National Park Rescue Team,° Estes Park, CO 80517 (Rocky Mountain National Park)

Rocky Mountain Rescue Group, Inc.,° PO Box Y, Boulder, CO 80306 (Colorado)

San Juan Mountain SAR, PO Box 4, Silverton, CO 81433

Summit County Rescue Group,° PO Box 1794, Breckenridge, CO 80424 (Summit County)

Vail Mountain Rescue Group,° PO Box 115, Vail, CO 81658

Western State Mountain Rescue Team,° Western State College, Gunnison, CO 81231

IDAHO
Idaho Mountain Search and Rescue,° PO Box 8714, Boise, ID 83707
Palouse-Clearwater Search and Rescue,° Route 1, Box 103-B, Troy, ID 83871

MAINE
Baxter State Park Mountain Rescue Team,° 64 Balsam Drive, Millinocket, ME 04462

MONTANA
Glacier National Park Rescue Service,° PO Box 636, Essex, MT 59916
Lewis and Clark Search and Rescue,° PO Box 473, Helena, MT 59601

NEW HAMPSHIRE
Appalachian Mountain Club, Pinkham Notch Camp, Gorham, NH 03581 (White
    Mountains)
Mountain Rescue Service,° PO Box 494, North Conway, NH 03860 (New Hampshire)

NEW MEXICO
Albuquerque Mountain Rescue Council,° PO Box 53396, Albuquerque, NM 87153
St. John's College Search and Rescue Team, PO Box 350, St. John's College, Camino
    de Cruz Blanca, Santa Fee, NM 87501 (Northern New Mexico, Southern
    Colorado)

NORTHWEST TERRITORIES
Auyuittuq Park Warden Service, Auyuittuq National Park, Pangnirtung, N.W.T. X0A
    0R0 (Auyuittuq National Park)

OREGON
Alpinees, Inc.,° 3571 Belmont Dr., Hood River, OR 97301 (Hood River County)
Corvallis Mountain Rescue Unit,° PO Box 116, Corvallis, OR 97339 (Central
    Cascades)
Crater Lake National Park Rescue Team, PO Box 7, Crater Lake, OR 97604 (Crater
    Lake National Park)
Eugene Mountain Rescue,° PO Box 10081, Eugene, OR 97401 (Oregon Cascades)
Hood River Crag Rates,° 1450 Nunamaker, Salem, OR 97031
Portland Mountain Rescue,° PO Box 1222, Portland, OR 97207

UTAH
American Search Dogs,° 4939 Benlomand, Ogden, UT 84003
Rocky Mountain Rescue Dogs,° 9624 S. 1210 E., Sandy, UT 84070
Salt Lake County Sheriff Search and Rescue,° 2942 Cardiff Road, Salt Lake City,
    UT 84121
Zion National Park°, Chief Ranger, Springdale, UT 84767

VERMONT
Mountain Cold Weather Rescue Team, Norwich University, Northfield, VT 05663

VIRGINIA
Appalachian Search and Rescue Conference°, PO Box 430, Flint Hill, VA 22627 (Blue Ridge and Shenandoah Mountains and Southwest Virginia)

WASHINGTON
Bellingham Mountain Rescue Council°, PO Box 292, Bellingham, WA 98225 (Whatcom County)

Central Washington Mountain Rescue Council°, PO Box 2663, Yakima, WA 98907 (Washington)

Everett Mountain Rescue Unit°, PO Box 2566, Everett, WA 98203 (North Central Cascades)

Mount Rainier National Park Rescue Team°, Longmire, WA 98397 (Mount Rainier National Park)

Mountain Rescue Council, Inc., PO Box 67, Seattle, WA 98111 (Washington)

North Cascades National Park Rescue Team°, 2105 Highway 20, Sedro Woolley, WA 98284

Olympic Mountain Rescue°, PO Box 4244, Bremerton, WA 98312 (Olympic Range, Cascades)

Olympic National Park Rescue Team°, 600 Park Ave., Port Angeles, WA 98362 (Olympic National Park)

Skagit Mountain Rescue Unit°, 128 4th St., Mount Vernon, WA 98273 (Northern Cascades)

Tacoma Mountain Rescue Unit°, 7910 "A" St., Tacoma, WA 98408 (Central Washington, Cascades, Olympics)

WYOMING
Grand Teton National Park Mountain Search and Rescue Team°, PO Box 67, Moose, WY 83012 (Grand Teton National Park)

Mountain Rescue Outing Club, University of Wyoming, Laramie, WY 82071 (Wyoming)

YUKON
Kluane Park Warden Service, Kluane National Park, Haines Junction, Yukon Y0B 1L0 (Kluane National Park)

MOUNTAIN RESCUE ASSOCIATION OFFICERS

Dick Brethers, *President*
2942 Cardiff Road
Salt Lake City, Utah 84121

Kevin Walder, *Vice President*
1408 Mountain Avenue
San Jacinto, California 92383

Tim Cochran, *Secretary*
P.O. Box 115
Vail, Colorado 81658

Louie H. Clem, *Executive Secretary*
Alpine Center for Rescue Studies
P.O. Box 1713
Idaho Springs, Colorado 80452

MOUNTAIN RESCUE ASSOCIATION, INC.
2144 South 1100 East-Suite 150-375
Salt Lake City, Utah 84106